JOURNEY BEYOND REASON

Fastest Man
Around the World

NICK SANDERS

ON THE ROAD
PUBLISHING

JOURNEY BEYOND REASON

Fastest Man
Around the World

NICK SANDERS

ON THE ROAD
PUBLISHING

An **On the Road Publication**
P.O. Box 27 Machynlleth Powys SY20 8WT
www.motochallenge.com
www.nicksanders.com
First published in Great Britain by **On the Road Publishing,** 2005

Set in 11/12pt Bembo
Layout by Joseph Alan at Y Lolfa
Jacket by Garry Mears
Jacket photograph by Chippy
Printed and bound in Great Britain by
Mackays, Chatham

ISBN 0 95490 811 2 Hardback
ISBN 0 95490 812 0 Softback

Acknowledgements

There will always be someone I've forgotten, names I didn't write down at the time, countless people who helped in small but important ways but I would like to thank the following sponsors and individuals without whom this short journey would not have happened.

Tony Robinson at Punctureseal International for his financial support along with Mark Gregory for his belief in the project and encouragement. Also Pete Littlewood at Webbs bike shop in Lincoln (as well as Rivetts) and his bosses Andre and Steve. Pete was brilliant with his enthusiasm, thanks to Julian for prepping the bike and also all the staff. Thanks also to Karen Milsom at Bennetts for their financial help.

Big thanks once again to Miles Taylor at Yamaha UK for the use of the 2005 YZF R1, one of the best bikes for the job! Patrick Keen and his boss Neville at Cambrian Tyres for use of their Continental Road Attacks. To Jon Hale at UK Biker for financial support and managing the web site. To Rob and Dave at Visual Impact Northern for their kind loan of the Z1 HD Sony TV camera. To Simon Wilkinson at the BMF. To Gerbings for the heated clothing, Chris Walker at Euro Helmets for the Wolf leathers and AGV helmets. Also to Joe Talbot and Dave Fewings at Men & Motors for supporting the filming. Big last minute thanks to Dave Marsden at Z Power for stepping into the breech as Executive Producer.

On a personal note I would like to thank Carrie for her text messages and photos which means she'll never be able to marry Prince William. Thanks to Jiten Suchede who flew into Abercegir from Delhi to man the office. Big thanks to Paul Blezard (Blez) for proofing and subbing this book (poor man!). Thanks to Steve Hughes for looking after the book keeping and fending off my creditors whilst I was away (which was one reason I went!). Thanks to my mates Cyco and Mike. Thank you to Elspeth, Jane and Sam for being really great pals and bailing me out of North America! Marco for occasionally driving me in the van to the border of Gurcistan whilst I finished off the book and also to Beatrice, my lovely ex mother-in-law who loaned me 200 euros on the last day in Benissa, without which, believe it or not, I wouldn't have got this record. And how could I miss out my ex-wife Hennie for looking after the kids, Tatty, JJ and Willow who will maybe one day break my record. And finally and especially to Roger Murray, one of my great friends, who has helped me with my ideas for 20 years, to whom this journey is dedicated.

Nick Sanders
East Turkey (Iranian border)
September 2005

To put the record straight

In 1997 I set the record for the Guinness Book of Records' *Speed Circumnavigation of the World*, riding 31 days and 19,381 miles. The previous year I had ridden from Tierra del Fuego to Alaska in 30 days as a training run. No one I knew had thought about doing an around the world bike record so it seemed left to me to give it a go, and even though I could have gone faster, the previous motorised record was 33 days, accomplished by three chaps in a car, so I planned only to beat them. I was going to attack my own record in 2001 and had positive negotiations with Guinness but I could not get ready that year. Then, in 2002 a husband and wife team rode a motorcycle around the world in under 20 days. Guinness were persuaded to disband the record, supposedly on the grounds of safety even though there are much more dangerous records and many precedents of motoring events with some risk in the public domain. This conveniently allowed the present record holders to keep their Guinness title in perpetuity since it could no longer be challenged.

I decided therefore to break my previous record, which was a solo journey and distinctly different from the rider and pillion one, but I thought I'd have a crack at breaking their record of 19 days and eight hours anyway.

For Roger Murray

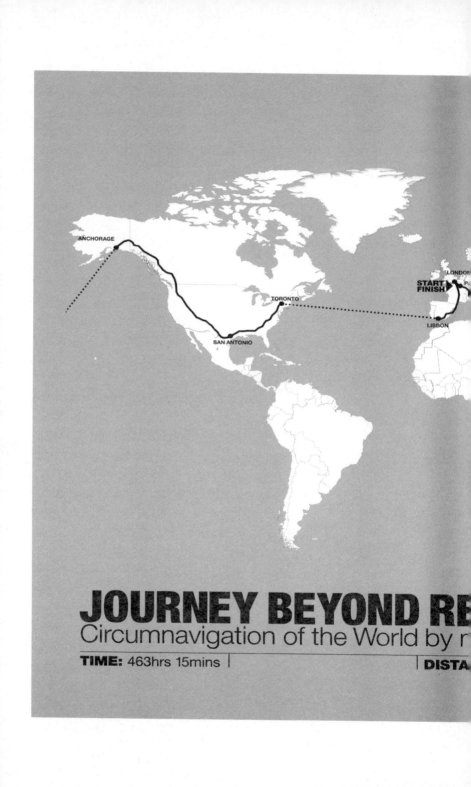

ANCHORAGE

TORONTO

SAN ANTONIO

LONDON

START
FINISH

P

LISBON

JOURNEY BEYOND RE
Circumnavigation of the World by r

TIME: 463hrs 15mins | | **DISTA**

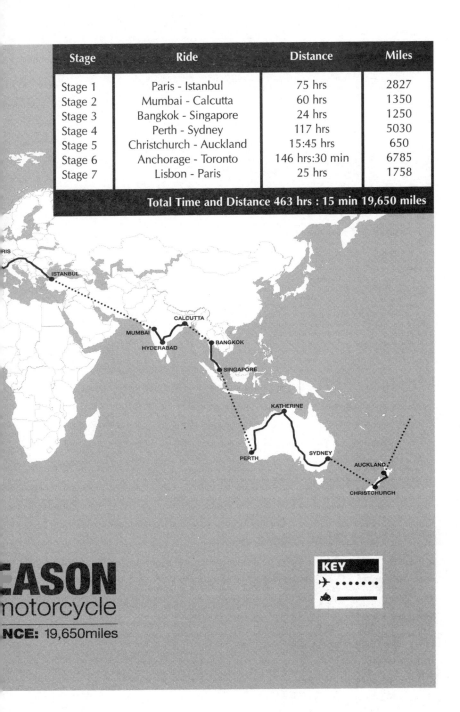

Stage	Ride	Distance	Miles
Stage 1	Paris - Istanbul	75 hrs	2827
Stage 2	Mumbai - Calcutta	60 hrs	1350
Stage 3	Bangkok - Singapore	24 hrs	1250
Stage 4	Perth - Sydney	117 hrs	5030
Stage 5	Christchurch - Auckland	15:45 hrs	650
Stage 6	Anchorage - Toronto	146 hrs:30 min	6785
Stage 7	Lisbon - Paris	25 hrs	1758

Total Time and Distance 463 hrs : 15 min 19,650 miles

EASON
motorcycle
NCE: 19,650miles

KEY
✈ • • • • • • •
🏍 ▬▬▬▬▬

THE BEGINNING

Everyone said I shouldn't go. No one thought it was a good idea that I try to motorcycle around the world faster than it had ever been done. Any journey around the world by motorcycle is hard, but this was going to be harder. I've ridden around the world fast and I've ridden around the world and taken my time, so I know the difference between the two ways of travelling. If you could start a journey like this knowing how you might feel at the end, it's possible you wouldn't go. If you knew what was involved and how much it would hurt before you left, then the screams of reason would have to be muffled by a type of madness before you could start your engine and go.

★ ★ ★ ★ ★

The planning of this journey had taken place in my head over several years but the packing took less than an hour. I'd previously thought I'd never ride so quickly around the world again, but something needled me to try to make this solo project more perfect as a concept than it had been before.

I had originally planned to ride down from Calais to Lisbon, but a last minute reflection made me think it better I went the other way round. East to west gives you added daylight time because of the way you chase the sun, but that also meant at dusk having to ride into the maddening glare of the sun precisely at eye-line which was equally hard riding.

Journeying west meant you often get a headwind, which in the winter seriously affects the wind chill but that wasn't what formed my decision. It was the fact that my ride across India happened earlier in the journey when I was still at my strongest. To tackle this continent in a weak condition is inviting disaster. This journey would attempt to cross India at the very peak of the summer just days before the monsoon and should the ride coincide with the rains, which are notoriously difficult to forecast precisely, then all would be lost.

The plan was to ride 18 hour days along places like the Grand Trunk Road which links Delhi to Bombay and is one of India's busiest highways. It was a while since I'd been there and vaguely remembered it being a place where traffic takes on the characteristic of a swarm of drowsy bees. One random out-of-control lorry at an unexpected moment was all that was needed for me to crash out of the project. If I were to fail, it wasn't an exaggeration to say that my core livelihood and house were at risk.

It could also be argued that I needed more time to get into a riding rhythm and that later, once travel-hardened to a greater degree you become capable of overcoming all obstacles. It was not easy to decide but in the end I opted for west–east. My assistant Jiten and I had changed the arrows on a world map several times and when I finally made the decision I suddenly felt unsure and really unprepared for the ride.

The bosses at Motor Cycle News had decided to send one of their journalists to follow me on day one. MCN had offered me three pages of their weekly publication, which was a huge amount of publicity so I biked down to Peterborough to make sure they were serious, and they were. As usual I was chided in a friendly way. The word 'mad' is misplaced and overused and is part of the price for being different. Certainly there was an element of the kettle calling the pot black as every motorcyclist enjoys a self determination bordering on strangeness. I took the epithet as a compliment, folded away my maps and said goodbye. We'd agreed that MCN's staff writer James Tindle would accompany me for the first day of

16

the Round the World attempt and write a feature about it.

It was dry on the way back to wherever I was going. The whereabouts of that evening's overnight was vague because I hadn't thought about where I was going to stay, although supper with my eccentric farmer friend near Sheffield was likely. I had planned to pick up a new bike from my dealer sponsor Webb's in Lincoln, but that would have to be put off to the following morning. Before that, I called into a pub near Worksop to sit down for a while. I wasn't particularly enthusiastic about my work. Like most people I was always paying off bills, running my business the best way I knew how. Money made me feel mortal and it's an easy thought to think of great journeys as somehow not needing to be linked to the normal laws of economics. In a twist of irony, it had been nearly 25 years since I had started to chase my fortune, and I was still as far from catching it as if I were just starting. It was a common knowledge that sometimes any consolidation of your career had to allow for a time when *'things come to you'*.

I did wonder if this journey was worth doing but then I always struggled with my journeys and whether they had any relevance to modern life. A journey like this was hardly a quick weekend away. Yet I was still fresh after all these years. Nothing had dampened my enthusiasm or sullied my affection for what I did. Likewise, the bike would have to react with the same level of spontaneity to survive. For example, because of the time of year I was scheduled to arrive in India, temperatures there would reach 45 degrees centigrade and tarmac would have begun to melt. Only the hardiest life forms move quickly in such conditions (if they move at all) and resting during the midday heat was simply not part of the plan. Yamaha's R1 activates its fan at 104 degrees centigrade, but I knew that leaving the engine running, stationary, without any constant stream of cooling breeze in a very hot place would take the bike's tolerance levels beyond the place road testers take them. Once, when my radiator ruptured 200 miles from anywhere somewhere in the Northern Territories, the clock registered 119 degrees and for a brief moment shot up to 127 until I shut down the machine. I had to wait for the whole block to cool before I could restart and ride another 10 miles, which is what I had to do six times an hour for the following eight hours. I stopped a car in the dead of night and two local blokes had some water and gave me a plastic can. Once they left me, not a single vehicle passed me for the rest of the night. It was unusually quiet.

With only two weeks to go before I was due to set off I went to see a few friends who would inspire me as my own energy and self belief were still lacking. Confidence is everything in such endeavours and 2004 had been a hard year; my marriage disintegrated shortly before I set off for a hard around the world group tour and by the Spring of 2005 I had not had a day off for months. Whenever I thought about my job as an adventurer, as a tour guide, as a writer or whatever, I always thought of the poor sods who humped potash down some heat-ridden volcano and died young. The comparison was onerous but it illustrated how relatively well off I was. Also, I still had my secret weapon; I was about to motorcycle around the world faster and simpler than I had ever done in my life. This journey would be conducted faster than anyone had ever taken a motor vehicle around the world before. I planned to take nothing with me except a video camera to record the journey. Definitely no luggage. My professional armoury included a very fast bike; the camera, documents and my leathers; nothing else. I wasn't going to carry any clothing other than under garments to soak up the sweat created by the leathers. These I planned to wash every night; fresh and tightly fitting underclothes – leggings and a tee shirt – made secure by my protective suit, gave me a feeling that if my body was held well in place, I would be prepared for any riding eventuality, even the possibility of a hard impact.

Budgeting for the project was a battle of nerves and even though I was well sponsored the costs of world transport had risen dramatically. Terrorist activity and the increased price of oil were partly to blame, but also, big journeys were being taken out of the hands of privateers like myself and placed into the hands of larger corporate players. However I had a series of highly motivated sponsors who were very keen that we got this project right. Tony was the boss of Punctureseal and enjoyed the reputation for keeping a trim sail on his financial excesses, but he was looking after me perfectly. Tall, debonair, courteous he was the ideal Captain of the team along with Mark, his number 2 who had masterminded my involvement with the company these past couple of years. Pete Littlewood at Webb's in Lincoln headed up my dealer network and Julian, their mechanic was drafted in to service the bike, which was, as usual, a YZF R1 supplied by Miles Taylor at Yamaha UK. Karen at Bennetts supported me financially as did Jon at UK Biker: Chris Walker provided me with Wolf leathers which were made from Kangaroo skin and were incredibly light. Patrick at Cambrian Tyres near Aberystwyth had supplies of Continental Road Attack tyres waiting for me all over the world, and Shirley at Yamaha's public relations agency Promark was helping out with the marketing. Jiten was to man the office back home in Wales, Big Steve was looking after my events later in the year whilst not-so-big Steve kept tabs on the company accounts. Somewhere in the background Hennie looked after our three children, while their silly Dad did what he had to do, as usual! So I was not entirely alone. Not only was this project important to me, it had become important to them and I didn't want to let anyone down.

After staying overnight with my old mate Bruce near Sheffield I rode over to Webb's where Julian had prepared the new bike. Pete was there, as usual, overseeing everything. I was to run in the bike personally, something I always insisted on doing and I rode back along the Snake Pass which descended down to Glossop, a small town where I had lived as a youth. My schedule for the day had been binned so I decided to ride gently and run my bike in and not exceed 5000 revs. I called into my office when Jiten said that there were more company problems that needed addressing. Money was now a key issue and I was forced to ride for reward as well as for my life. Only a successful completion of this journey would turn things around.

My scattergun attitude to making money was a hair's breadth from becoming my nemesis. I didn't have a lot of spare capital but that's all right as long as you've got a good plan. In all adventures there is a prologue that catalogues the fortunes of the brave and the impecunious. As I was only too aware, this project was a hostage to fortune. Also, I was just the same as most people, exposed like them to the myth of freedom. Freedom is a state of mind and I was not the free man I was supposed to be. The moment the record attempt ended I was supposed to lead ten riders to Transylvania and the moment I got back from that I was scheduled to be in the editing studio to cut the film. Only after that could I look forward to some free time in August with my kids but in the evenings when they were asleep, I would have to write my book. After that it was back on the bike: London to the Iranian border with 15 riders and a day after getting back from that I was to take 23 riders around the coast of Britain. Finally, I would be going to Morocco for a week with my last group of the year.

After riding into Glossop, a once quiet back water east of

Manchester, my head filled with memories. I remember my Dad standing on the step of his house asking me why I was always so busy. When I told him that 'busy is good', he said that ants had the same policy. I was too busy to bother with an answer and shot off on my bike, but loopholes in time bring back such things to haunt you. The fastest man journey which I conceived and rode nearly ten years ago was, as a process, in part a carbon copy of this journey. It allowed me to ride faster, longer, better and safer than before because more of the complexities of the journey were known. The psychological make-up of the journey however remained the same. What the voice in my head said to me then, applied now:

Fastest Man Extract (1997)

"Why is this record so important to you?"

"I don't know. I can't help myself. Something inside me won't let me stop."

"Perhaps it's some psychological need which refuses to be fulfilled."

"Maybe I suffer from grey dogs in my head, classical morbidity, which I strive to overcome. Maybe I do it because I just want to do it."

"It's a curse."

"Yes, it is," I said.

"No balance or moderation."

"Last night I dreamed of darkness. I was a small boy. I was alone. My dad had gone and that small boy closed his eyes tightly and his body began to compact into a heaviness so huge that it collapsed under its own weight. He was suddenly smaller than a pin head and unable to move. His eyelids were heavier than the moon."

Adaptation is simply a process which means you've figured out how to survive in the world. If you are a passionate motorcycle rider it probably transforms you into a two-wheeled 'warrior' at least once a week. Seven days a week is quite a test but the change of mind-set is similar. A man who might be a clerk living a hum-drum life away from his bike becomes John Wayne when he steps astride his machine. His bike is his war-horse and instead of riding down the M1 he sees only tumbleweed as he looks across the plains. My situation is more extreme but it is a myth to suggest that all you have to do is ride very fast to get around the world in 19 days. In theory, all you have to do is ride at 50 mph for 20 or so hours a day and rest when the bike is being shipped. I didn't know it then, but riding fast, 24 hours a day for days at a time without sleep and only the slimmest of margins to fuel, lubricate, feed, water and empty the bike and the body was still not the whole truth. Getting around a thousand corners quickly whilst simultaneously watching a selection of surfaces all of which if misinterpreted could kill you, is but another underrated riding skill you need to have; but it's not just that, as every single item of road furniture, millions of them, must all be avoided. Technically, as you learn to instantly recognise different traffic patterns, it's more than this. You also begin to 'download' life information into smaller bits, with especial reference to road information that breaks it down into something less chunky. One aspect of my life surely had something to do with whittling the world down to a more manageable size. With this in mind, I rode a bike, but it was only the road that changed, everything else more or less remained the same.

Journeys like this require a certain amount of self-knowledge. My technique was to write myself into my own screenplay, because it was too complex for me to write about anyone else. It's true that a man who has the common sense to say nothing, if he has nothing to say, is wise indeed but most of us talk too much and few of us have anything really important to say. The world is full of opinions. After twenty-five years of travelling I had either become very stupid, or else become a person who has no reason to know anything about life other than his place in it. It was precisely this known place; the hole that the jigsaw piece fits into, that gave me enough quirky stability to really believe I could do it, that I could bike around the world faster than anyone else. In this context, there are three types of people; those that think they know where they are going and those that don't, and those who don't think who reckon it doesn't matter. I just wanted to give it a go, ask myself what it was that made me do these adventures and pass on the little that I knew.

It was definitely a compulsion. In my head there is a terrible gnawing need that drags you from your life in such a way that nothing matters more than a journey. Sometimes I thought of *'the journey'* as an organic being. It was like looking down the wrong end of a telescope at something which had a life of its own. *'The journey'* was also a metaphor for freedom, emancipation, the meaning of life and it was all centred around the simple act of riding your very own time and space machine. A motorcycle takes you to faraway places where time is sometimes faster or slower. There are places in the world where ox carts have not yet been replaced by combustion engines, and there are other places where people never feel the heat of the sun on their back because there is a corridor of air-conditioning that connects them from their bed to their office and back. The person guiding the ox has probably worn the same clothes for months, the other is looking for the slightest sign of a sweat stain before he has his shirt cleaned and pressed.

So strong is the concept of moving, it gives the impression that it has its own independent existence. If you could personify the concept of *moving*, it might be as a hypnotist willing you to do something out of character. Either you discover a sense of enlightenment, or you just bark like a dog. Either way you risk being sucked away from your former life, automatically removed from any responsibility for what you are leaving behind. The further you go, the more self–centred you become and the faster you slide down an emotional helix which involves less responsibility to others and an increasing reliance on yourself. Without this tie to home, you eventually ride so far away you start to become forgotten; it is just you and your shiny motorbike, the sound of your own breathing and the furious tapping of valves that let in fuel and release exhaust. It is the bike and the *journey* that allow you to cast off restraint and immerse yourself solely in your dream and return a hero. Jason and his Argonauts were dreamers and they came back heroes, no doubt alienated because dreaming does not fit into the paradigm of a pragmatic life. Anyone can do *dreaming*, it's just that if you act upon it, you have to be prepared for the consequences. There is a gulf between these two kinds of reality, dreaming and not dreaming, and it is the hardest gap to cross. Like not being able to wake, you cannot stop dreaming. Instead of settling payments for your utility bills, you want instead to stretch out in the sun having ridden across Asia Major. Why return to earth when you can park up near the North Pole and bathe in shadows; where, sitting by your bike you can watch comets crash through a magnetic sky knowing you are as close to riding across a world with two suns as any astronaut.

By visualising the route you become a symbol of worldliness; catching the ferry by the Shell garage at Dover's Eastern Docks you ride off the ramparts at Terminal Routier du Port Ouest. There's a girl in a Norfolk Line uniform whom you'd like to take with you but you know it would never work out so you get on the A26 and before long you are jousting with the cars on Paris's peripherique. Exiting at Port d'Orléans you head away from the sun and while it's not as exotic as flying over the Sahara or sailing on the Caspian Sea, it's worth noting that from the point of view of the record, the journey has just been born.

Not the ideal preparation...

I'd been ill all week with a bug the kids had given me and I was plagued with sleepless nights. Worries about money, about writing the book and I didn't really know how it was going to be possible to single-handedly shoot the film. I didn't tell anybody at the time but I had no idea how I would find time to ride a motorbike round the world in 18 or 19 days and still get all my jobs done. There was no margin for error, yet I didn't think I was lucky or perfect enough to get it absolutely right. That night I'd worked late and in an hour or so it would begin to get light. I sat quietly looking out of the window as the night began to melt away. A crack of dawn appeared across the soft Welsh hills that could be seen through my office window. I sat there and just hoped that things would kind of work out. Often, your head solves difficult problems when you stop thinking about them and, in a make-believe world, you wake up and everything's perfect again. There are times when doing nothing is the best thing to do and sometimes it's the worse thing; the trick is knowing when to do what.

The only way out of my depression, caused by my self-doubt, was to crack back into the sanctuary of my own screenplay. The settings were harbours, hotels, airports, trains and railway station waiting rooms. These were my safe homes and the journey was my safety blanket. For twenty five years they were the places in the world where I felt happy and comfortable and just when I thought it was safe to emerge out of character, I panicked and retreated back into my professional obsession. It was here where brief insights came to me after years of hard compressed moments of reflection. I never thought of this journey having a start and an end, although technically it did, but really, the overall project was simply something that was planned to fit into my early summer schedule; somewhere between trips to Alaska and Turkey; somewhere between making and losing money and definitely somewhere between being scared and excited, both at the same time, whilst wanting, and yet not wanting to do it. Once the seed of an idea takes root, I never gave myself a choice; it had to be carried out and whilst less painful than giving birth, it was no less unstoppable once it started. So entrenched was this idea of *continuum*, that in brief quiet moments, everything appeared matter-of-fact. Yet such was the force needed to even think about the journey that most of the time it left my head bruised. This was, after all, simply a journey that included a world record attempt on a motorcycle with the soubriquet of *'fastest man around the world'*.

Nothing is straightforward in the mental planning of such a journey. It was fuelled by some edgy fission at the cost of a life of servitude to the idea of being the best at something you did passionately. This need to strive was only part of what it was all about. Every motorcycle mechanic who strips down an engine, who takes out this or that valve and spring, who polishes and hones and then rebuilds it until it sounds like a musical instrument, operates in a similar way. The pursuit of perfection or at least a job well done was another part of the reason to go and it meant another part of the answer lay elsewhere and was something only the journey might solve.

On the Thursday I left the kids to watch a video while I briefly went down to my office in order to speak to my Indian friend Jiten. He had flown over from Delhi to run my business while I would be on the road later in the year. He was very self-motivated and made me feel relaxed about leaving him with such a responsibility until I got back. For just over a year I had run my company single-handedly and since March of 2004 there had been no-one in my office except me. As well as sticking on the stamps I had also to think of the ideas. It's not that the ideas were so big, it was simply that I hadn't got any that were bigger. Going around the world and sometimes taking people with me was about as big as it got. My wife Hennie and I had split up and while we missed each other terribly – well, I missed her anyway – I was also trying to be a full-time dad to our three kids when I had them for nearly half the year. As well as being a motorcyclist, I had to be what my father had been to me and tried to be both mum and dad to them. I kept the business going by working late in the evenings, after bedtime stories, and wrote my books before porridge time. It was as much as I could do to tread water, only just keeping my head above the surface. Money was key and if I had to ride around the world only for the glory I wouldn't go. I'd recently lost three Alaska riders because of their last-minute personal problems, and had to cancel a project around Britain and another across the Himalayas through lack of interest. The cash had to come in from somewhere, but where?

More of my nights were spent sleepless as the real worry about my financial situation took a grip. The fact that I was ill with a chest infection and that the nurse had recently found blood in my urine only compounded the panic. My customary huge energy had deserted me and it made me slow to the point where my chest froze and made me feel I wasn't breathing. My heartbeat was different, the force and rhythm were not there. Having been ill for ten days, it took the next day for me to realise that the malady might have been the result of stress or overwork or even stage nerves but significantly it was also the cause of my inability to get well. It wasn't letting me get better; this slight illness had stopped my training in its tracks. Six weeks before I was due to start the record ride I couldn't run more than 20 steps before feeling too weak to stand. I was too ill to ride my bike. If it's true that you can think yourself well, then illness counters this by creating a mindset that allows it to flourish. The virus was eating away at my will to do things. This illness wanted to drive me into stillness so it could feed off my spirit. Years of experience should have been reassurance enough but even that way of thinking was temporarily corrupted. It felt like my life was out of control and I needed something to wrench it back again.

As a child I had gone to bed early and as a young man I had looked after myself well. Home life had not been happy and sleep had been my rescue. The regime of bicycle racing gave me geographical freedom and took me as far from my family as I could reasonably get without leaving home. I had endured this for years and became tough but also healthy. This developed huge stores of energy in me, stored in a battery that was in tip-top shape. If I ever drained myself to some extreme limit, my recovery rate was rapid and a quick overnight charge was all that was needed to keep me on the road. I didn't know any more than the next person and didn't feel particularly skilled, but those reserves of energy and the single-mindedness it fed, had become the vital components that were to separate me from most people.

For weeks leading up to the start I sat at home, the kids tucked up in bed, alone as usual on a Saturday night. I had become used to living in my head and I imagined my life just then as if it were looking for a ghost orchid which, in its fantastic, fleeting and bewilderingly secret place, was still too precious to pick. Every orchid has a particular shape to receive a particular insect, and when that insect lands it makes love to the plant in such a way that it takes the pollen to another and creates a bigger world. When looking at his fauna during his voyages in HMS Beagle, Charles Darwin saw an orchid of such a shape that he hypothesised there must be something with a nine-inch proboscis in order that it might mate. Everyone derided him, but he was right, there was that animal in the shape of an ant-eater with a nine inch proboscis. I was unembarrassed about passion and this analogy about the perfect fit between people or places which you never think can happen, has to, or something you want very badly will never become true.

★ ★ ★ ★ ★

Yamaha's press people, headed by Shirley Patterson, were doing all they could and so far various TV stations had filmed me along with big papers like the Manchester Evening News and the London Evening Standard. The headline exposure that I really needed continued to elude me, yet there were rumblings of real interest. The core value of my audience was growing as the number of visitors looking at the website had quadrupled to 4000 people a day. In fact, the whole campaign was running very smoothly and with more control would hit small but solid peaks exactly as planned. It's a simple fact that it is always easier to promote a project that has run to its conclusion than one that hasn't started. The strategy to engage thousands of motorcyclists to read about my events was working, that was the easy part; what was now required was a mechanism to engage people to ride with me on some of my journeys.

The day I relaxed with my children

Nothing much happened except that it was a hot summer's day. Small white clouds drifted lazily by and my babies wandered about sweetly with such wonderful purpose, but which made sense only to them. There were no butterflies, no bullfrogs croaking, not even a harsh heat that slowed everything to no movement. It was special only because I had my family in the palm of my hand. My eldest boy understood what was happening and was nervous but the other two were oblivious to what my leaving really meant. For a few brief hours I lay in worship of my only really important achievements: my children. Hennie had left me because of my total commitment to creating the *perfect* adventure. It took up my time and took me away from home and eventually, even great love cracks.

Meanwhile, Jiten was working in the office. We talked about various press releases, the final examination of the route and an analysis of what results we should expect from the project. For me, the Yamaha R1 was the best bike I could ever have. To an art lover it was a Da Vinci painting, to a master craftsman it was a Stradivarius violin. For me, it was a bike that I could position exactly where I wanted it and keeping me alive was the greatest gift it could give me. Whenever I expected it to slip it never did, when the back end waggled because of over-braking into a corner it always straightened up. Whenever it was in mid air it always landed back on the ground in an upright position. Having ridden 100,000 miles and three times around the world on two R1s, I was poised to do it again with even better awareness of its handling characteristics.

Jiten had spent the weekend cycling around the area and down to the coast, I had ventured no further than the town and the edge of my land. The sunshine made the green more green and the rolling Welsh hills looked as warm and soft as velvet. If there was ever a place I wanted to be, it was here when the sun shone, in this tiny little valley with its small group of incomers alongside the friendly locals. Friends Paddy and Paul ran the bed and breakfast at the bottom of the track and had organised a going away breakfast for me later in the week. Wendy and Ian were off to Canada for a holiday, Scott and Sara were somewhere in New York state, Tony cycling to Mexico and I was off around the world and for the first time from here, the west coast of Britain. It wasn't that people here were any more insular than anywhere else, but because of the distance that separated us from large conurbations of industry and people, we felt less part of the mainland, side-lined from mainstream life.

There were a few things that I had left to organise in order that I could start in a couple of weeks' time. I knew my paperwork wouldn't let me down. I'd already spoken to my freighters in Istanbul and they were talking to Bombay and Calcutta. The carnet would be sent from the RAC mid week and my passport had just been sent back from the Indian Embassy with a new entry visa. We were down to the small detail. The sponsors provided the capital and the bikes and the PR people were slowly beginning to reap a return on their investment.

7th May 2005

Two weeks to go and I am feeling excited but very nervous. A lot of the preparation is still ongoing and I think we'll all be down to the wire if we are to be ready in time. The new bike is excellent and after 700 miles riding it is just starting to loosen up. I'm at 6000 revs and you can feel the machinery 'giving' – the whole bike is starting to feel more playful. Pete at Webb's in Lincoln has engineered everything to do with the bike and for weeks has been busy sorting out the servicing and preparation. We tried unsuccessfully to have the fuel tank enlarged because with only 18 litres I would have to start looking out for fuel after 100 miles. At best, riding very gently, the R1 can have a range of 200 miles, but at speed the reserve light comes on at anything between 125 and 135 miles, allowing for only another 15 to 30 mile before it runs dry. Pete made an early decision to build a rear tank which could only be positioned over the pillion seat. It sounded an inspired move but I was apprehensive at how an extra 12 litres lying relatively high would affect the handling of the bike. I went into Webb's the other day and Julian set out to do the servicing. The bike only really needed an oil and filter change but he checked everything, tightened the chain, looked at all the fluids and generally gave it a clean bill of health. Once the project starts I'll have no time at all to engage in anything other than the riding. I'll be alone with no one else out there to help. In fact, my one and only service is scheduled to take place in Perth, Australia.

After my village send-off, Steve loaded the bike into the van and drove me to the showground near Peterborough where the BMF were saying goodbye at a more official level. Personally I would have liked to slip away without anyone noticing, not dissimilar to the way my Dad used to quietly get on with his life. He would often tell me some cliché or relate some word of wisdom garnered through years of enduring life. Like him, I am not altogether comfortable with the company of other people. In some ways this honed my focus because once gone, it wouldn't matter whether I came back: this was the frame of mind I was getting myself in to.

The day before I left

In the Harvesters Pub, a stone's throw from the rally site, myself, the lads from my main sponsor Punctureseal, Carrie and Jiten sat and enjoyed a good meal. I still hadn't packed for the journey and some technical elements associated with the bike still had to be resolved. The rear petrol tank that Pete had organised wasn't suitable due to its size and the fact that it was positioned too close to where I was seated and would be in constant contact with the movie camera I was carrying on my back. Still, we'd got most of it right. Most projects don't get off the drawing board and even more stumble at the last hurdle. At least this adventure was going to make it to the start line and that was an achievement in itself. I was feeling good, quite composed, a little nervous but perfectly focused. In my head I was beginning to entertain the idea that the record was achievable. I was riding well, had trained at speed, felt more refreshed than I had for weeks and had gained real control over my financial problems. The small publicity machine surrounding the project had worked well, the team around the project were keen and capable and whilst I knew it was soon going to be down to me, everyone now felt confident that their efforts were not going to be in vain.

THE JOURNEY STARTS

I left Calais at 10.45 on the Monday and arrived in Istanbul at 18.00 local time on the Thursday. Extrapolating the time differences, that equates to 3 days and _ of an hour. It was only later that I decided to shift the start and finish point to Paris. As I rode 2980 miles, one divided into the other would give me a little under 1000 miles each day. I was on schedule, or at least so close that it would not be too difficult to eliminate this difference. The idea of not sleeping on the journey had never occurred to me, as I assumed that regular patterns of behaviour would keep my reserves sustained over a longer period. By riding almost non stop for over three days I had stayed on schedule. I had decided to operate this journey as a series of stages, to run along the same rules and regulations as those required by the Guinness Book of Records even though I knew that they would no longer ratify my record. They seemed to think it was too dangerous to want to record a journey like this, and the rebel in me didn't care. I would now ride from Bombay to Calcutta non-stop and had made a mental note to cover the 1350 or so miles in around 60 hours, substantially less than the 4 days it took me in 1997. It was becoming clearer to me that the difference between then and now, and why I should be capable of such reductions in time, was simply that I was now a far better rider than before. Back then, I had only just started riding a fast bike and was brave but hopelessly lacking in experience. Subsequent to that journey nine years ago I had ridden around the world a further three times and this journey was my sixth motorcycle circumnavigation, and eighth if you include the cycling. All those journeys meant that I was comfortable travelling the world on two wheels; there was nothing to really distract or trouble me. In 1997 I thought I was a good rider but I was wrong. Only now had I become the rider I really needed to be.

12.19hrs GMT, 23rd May

We (that's James Tindle from MCN and me) left Calais at 10:45, we didn't get in to Calais until 2:00 in the morning from London for all sorts of reasons. We left at 10:45 from the Hotel Bellville in the centre of Calais . We took the A26 autoroute, then the A1 and now within two hours we are near Paris . The bike is going very well, I am riding it at about 6000 revs. I am feeling absolutely fine, really good. Feeling very focused and I think the journey is going to go very well. If I carry on with this schedule, I will easily reach 1200 miles in the first 24hrs, maybe more…so we'll see how we are going to do. The route I am planning for the next 24hrs is Paris, south to Lyon, south east to Monaco then north east towards Geneva, and then to Regensburg and onto Prague. The weather is good. Light clouds, blue sky, traffic not too heavy. I am very glad to be actually on the road. No problems at all and I am hoping to make to Istanbul within two and a half days.

18.59hrs GMT, 23rd May

When I was riding down from 7500 to 6500 revs, I suddenly realised there was a tremendous vibration in the front wheel, and I didn't know what it was. It was as if the bike had hit a serrated road. I don't know what it was. It has now happened a second time, so I am a little bit wary. I seem to be adjusting to the bike reacting differently because the riding has become quite extreme. At 483 miles, I actually started to fall asleep and drifted very close to a truck so I stopped for a power nap. What was interesting about the power nap which I used to use in 1997 was that a 15 minute rest refreshed me for several hours, and I was a bit concerned that this technique might not work for me anymore, now that I am a bit older. But it has worked and I am feeling fantastic. We've done about 550 miles and are now south of Lyon and on our way to Marseille, on the A6 moving onto the A7. Am feeling really good and am now going to do the next 6 hours, which will take me up to midnight.

21.19hrs GMT, 23rd May

I am in Marseille. I am just about to start riding through the night.

It's full moon, so it's quite well lit. It's dry. I am riding well. I don't feel like a second power nap. I am feeling good. The bike is behaving very well. The idea now is to go along the Cote d'Azur, which is…from Marseille to Nice to Monaco . Then I'll start heading north over the Alps up to Regensburg. We have now ridden 680 miles.

14.48hrs GMT, 24th May
We've done 1383 miles and ridden non-stop for 26 hours. I am now in southern Germany , having left Innsbruck in Austria we are now on the A12 heading towards Regensburg where I leave James; then I head alone further east to Prague which is another 400 miles to ride. Am aiming for a total of 1800 miles, which will be in a time of 34 hrs. I am feeling very good. Bike is going well. Going to be riding until 9.00pm tonight.

James was to report on the first day's ride. He rode well and for 24 hours he was my only company. I had planned to be in Regensburg in southern Germany at the end of this time and we were less than an hour later than planned. Such an unexpectedly accurate reflection of my scheduling gave me a quiet confidence. He and I sat in a café in one of the small main squares of Regensburg. James was quiet. I assumed he was tired, but maybe he was suffering from disillusionment because the ride hadn't lived up to his expectations or he was experiencing a temporary reality shift. He had never ridden this way before and it must have been odd when the ride came to an abrupt end. After a quick beer I said goodbye and rode off in the direction of the motorway which would take me directly to Prague. He would stay that night in a hotel and make his way home the following day.

Fastest Man Extract (1997)
I was past Dijon within the hour, whisking along the autoroute with abandon. I felt strong and fit. The bike sounded good, held the road

well and faced into the wind sturdily. Sweet-smelling rapeseed pollen occasionally floated across the autoroute, and the truest yellow stretched against the bluest sky in a marriage of colour. The wind plundered thoughts from my helmet as it sucked out the air. The roar of the wind mixed with the vigorous noise of my engine. From the autoroute I caught glimpses of plaits of rapeseed not yet unfurled, farmers hosing down terraces of ripening vines, or sitting beneath terracotta eaves sipping their wine. I felt happy. In my imagination I sat and drank with the farmers, dozy in the quiet air. By the time the afternoon light had curdled I was bloated with the day's efforts and aching as I reached Aix en Provence.

That late afternoon it was sunny and as the light melted into a dry and warm early evening, the capitol of the Czech Republic came into view. All the traffic seemed to be going in the same direction and the centrum signs gave me an indication that finding the city centre was not going to be hard. When I reached the river I stopped. The lack of time at my disposal was always going to be my enemy and accepting such compromises was part of the pact you make with a journey when you travel so fast. On the River Vitava, various river boats motored along and the effect they had against the dusky sky gave a strong impression that, unlike the River Thames in London, this river was used well by the city.

I hung around for a short while when a small wiry chap turned up with tattoos on his arm and a slightly seedy air. I thought he was waiting for a moment when I might become distracted and try and run off with something, but in fact he wanted to sell me cocaine and showed me a little packet wrapped in the way old fashioned razor blades were once sold separately. He didn't seem a bad man, just confused when he realised he wasn't going to make an immediate sale.

01.46hrs GMT, 25th May

I have ridden 1653 miles in the last 34 hours and have another 1000 miles to go through the night, from Prague to Bratislava to Budapest and across Romania and Bulgaria to Istanbul. I am hoping to sleep on the doorstep of friends of mine in Budapest because I am arriving there at 03.00 in the morning...their mum has left me a blanket. I'll plan to sleep for 3 hours before going onto Istanbul. It makes me think my journey is the exact opposite of the 'Long Way Round' and its multi- million dollar budget. I am on day 2, and I am already running out of money! ... but I am thinking of interesting ways to make the whole thing continue. Jiten has just told me that we might not be able to fly the bike out of India because of the 'dangerous goods' classification and the regulations at Calcutta customs. What are we going to do? He says he is going to try to pull some strings with his friends back in India and see if there is anyway around this, but what if not? What if we just technically cannot do it? I've just thought of a `Plan B'. I fly my bike from Istanbul to Bangkok, it'll take 3-4 days. In the meantime I will fly to Mumbai from where I rent and continue to ride an Enfield from Mumbai to Calcutta , while my R1 is being freighted to Bangkok. One way or another, the journey will continue.

That night I rode on the motorway to Budapest, some 300 miles from Prague. I talked a lot to myself that night and spent a fortune calling people on the phone. I thanked Roger for being such a great friend – the man who has guided me through my ideas these past 20 years. I spoke to my wife and told her how much I appreciated her looking after our children so I could complete this journey. In fact, as I passed Brno, I was a thoroughly nice guy. If someone had suggested just then that I was the guy who, having tried to catch two rabbits had caught neither, I would have admitted to my over-full life being the cause of my many failures. I wanted more than anything just to be simple in spirit. I rode over the Danube at Bratislava as people were just beginning to wake.

When I reached Budapest, people were going to work and I was going to call in to see my friends Emese and Gabor. I had planned to be there in the early hours but it was just past breakfast when I eventually arrived, so there was no time for a rest, only for a cup of tea. I chatted with Emese and her husband before setting off to ride across the rest of Hungary before entering Romania. This time across Europe I was destined not to sleep. How different this journey was to the first time I rode fast around the world when there was a less urgent desire in the air:

Fastest Man Extract (1997)
Thoughts before the following morning
I am in my bed at night. I have not yet woken. I hear the sound of wind against the eaves and imagine I see tumbleweed flicked against the window panes. Nothing inspires me to wake, to get on my bike and ride another day, nothing; except that as my eyes twitch I know I have a heart that sags without a quest. I snore quietly. My breath shows in the cold air of my dream and I sing in my sleep about the lilies where love once fed and remember soft secret smiles. I cherish their taste like milk. In my suspended consciousness I know that she is now far away. I am not me but a spirit carried by strange winds.

Unlike thoughts that I had in the fastest man journey, this journey had no emotional schedule. Such thoughts take time to digest and increasingly for me, this was a commodity in short supply. I continued along the road to Szeged which was a two lane highway and slow. The vehicle content was high and the average speed worryingly low. Because of the lack of four lane trunk routes it was impossible to record quick riding times in these parts. The same was true right across Romania. What investment they did make to their infrastructure was most obviously not in their roads which, whilst remarkably not pot-holed, were still very badly surfaced. Roads in

Romania are a patchwork of holes covered with black plasters of tarmac. Sometimes the plasters are plastered and all bridges needed more caution than normal to cross quickly. Often I felt my rear shock compress almost to bottoming out before rebounding and lifting the rear wheel off the ground with the released inertia. In a series of ultra fast movements, the tyres were not getting the kind of traction a bike like this normally enjoyed; it did settle but only after some micro-seconds in the air and when the bike returned to traction and did this many times each minute it made for a lively ride. As a real life road test this was the ultimate assessment for a sports bike. It occurred to me that once in India the R1 would be one of the very few in its style and class to be ridden there, and probably unique in the way I was planning to ride it. An obscure 'first' perhaps, but it shows the different nature of this project. Most people wouldn't consider the R1 suitable for this kind of adventure; I was going to make them think differently.

In Sibiu, a small city in the heart of Transylvania and at the foot of the Carpathian Meridonal, I sat and enjoyed my first brief rest stop of the day. Storm clouds were gathering in the direction I intended to ride as dusk fell. A grey white day turned dark blue and began to blacken and still there were 800 miles yet to ride to get to Istanbul and already I had been awake for two full days and nights. A final night of torrential rain in the dark surrounded by trucks on a two lane highway in the mountains was something I'd prefer not to have to do. While a bad day on the bike is better than a good day at work, this was stretching the point. Having put on my over-suit and repacked my camera and documents in plastic bags, I set off, at which point the heavens opened. Big juicy droplets of rain fell noisily and plentifully and visibility was low. Entering the mountains everything was dark and there was little to see of the scenery. Only by craning my neck upwards and to one side could glimpses of the steep nature of the pass be caught, and it was here where the mountains poked into the unforgiving sky. Several times my back wheel slipped and due to the volume of rain, it was hard to see anything other than the brake lights of the truck in front as they flickered at every corner. The liquid display on my instrument panel rarely went above 30 miles per hour and when it sunk to 26 so did my heart. By miss-planning this ride to cross such territory at night, it become immediately clear that I was going to lose a lot of time. The weather could not be pre-planned and in the end I settled into a safe rhythm based on 'damage limitation' rather than making progress. Had I retired sensibly to an inn I would have lost even more time, maybe a further six or seven hours, so I plodded on like a race horse trying to raise a canter across a turnip field.

Blinkered by steep walls and sandwiched between trucks for 12 hours, it was two in the morning before I decided to rest and take in some food, just as a place came into view. There were a few people being served and when I turned up, apart from a few unshaven men drinking and a table full of adolescent boys, the restaurateur stood before me laughing and wearing the shortest of skirts. I praised the Lord that I should be visited by such a sight, and although her body was a touch lumpy she had a fine pair of legs. What wouldn't I have done to wrap them around me in a nice warm bed? Instead, I simply admired them from a distance while she rustled me up a little something from the kitchen. Within an hour she was sitting next to me, mobile phone numbers exchanged with her wanting an invitation to Wales. And all in Romanian without a word of English. It wasn't that I wanted to make a hasty retreat but I had to because whilst she might have been kind to me, time was not so forgiving. By three in the morning the black clouds were dumping their load of rain again, making surface conditions treacherous and delaying the arrival of daylight. Sitting on my bike in the rain, alone on the side of the road, I was beginning to feel ill. It was a very uncomfortable vibration in my body that was a degree or so less tremulous than shaking and still I had at least 12 hours more to ride. Forcibly being kept awake against a back drop of severe fatigue is a known method of torture. Riding for two and a half days with no sleep must be a kind of self harm. As the comfort zone diminishes to the point when it is nearly not there, that is the time when ambition overrides sanity. When it did get light, the rain stopped and I power napped for a few minutes which made me feel immediately better. All I had to do was cross Bulgaria and even though I didn't stop for breakfast my spirits rose and the tremors stopped.

Bulgaria came and went and soon I crossed the border into Turkey at Svilengrad and reached the motorway to Edirne and onto Istanbul where my friend Ikbal was to meet me on the outskirts of the city.

Ikbal's dad Paolo Volparo was the most influential man in Turkish motorcycling. He was also my friend. I met him years ago in Gocek and slept on his boat. He was a sometime advertising executive who had lived in Rome and as well as being a theological publisher, he had also studied to be a priest. Like my friend Roger Murray, they shared world views which to me made sense. Neither was concerned with narrow minded attitudes and their philosophical windows were both studded with a great magnitude of experience. Advice from friends like this cannot be bought but earned on the path to enlightenment. Everyone has their guru, and these were mine.

I stayed briefly with Paolo. He compared me to the mythological characters you read about in the history books. He said I was a hero like Jason and that the Argonauts were my team and I refuted this as nonsense and rebuked him for his flattering comments. I told him that anyone can do what I do, it's just that in the pursuit of 'fullness of life', you must be prepared to die. If the process of motorcycling around the world so quickly has, because of its rarity, a purity, it is a journey through life which leads you by the hand almost more than you want to live.

After coffee and biscuits we said goodbye. It was too short and as Ikbal drove me to the airport, it was touch and go as to whether I'd make my flight. Traffic eased however and we were on the right side of the city to reach the departure terminal so I checked in two minutes before the counter closed.

In the late afternoon I looked out through corridors of glass at planes that were so huge and complicated it was a wonder they could move a few yards let alone fly six and a half miles in the sky over Arabia. When it did take off, over houses and people watching television whilst others made cups of tea, it became clear that until a certain height you can see the minutest detail, and as we rose higher over Istanbul, people could still be made out doing simple things like pruning their privet hedge. Cars were moving silently and to destinations I could already see. Watching life from a plane is almost like looking into the future. Should that motorist be in danger of an ambush, I would know first. Instead I saw only ladies in hats, who, sitting around swimming pools only became animated when one blew away in the wind. The plane became an inverse symbol of the journey, capable of doing all the things my bike couldn't. With a following wind and a dry surface any sports bike and good rider can get to the end of a runway without being completely out classed, but what then? The bike was faster and easier than bicycling or walking and in the time it takes to walk a mile, a motorcycle can cross a county. Maybe it's just part of the relativity principle because in the same time a plane can cross a country, a spaceship can circle the earth.

Alchemy was the ancient and somewhat unscientific form of chemistry whereby certain elements could supposedly be changed, including lead into gold. A plane changes the way we are. A plane carries with it the traces of all the lands and seas it crosses before it reaches the clouds – above which it has been suggested that at night it also takes in the stars. It is also a vehicle that provides us with an imaginative counterweight. After all, if you have an adventurous spirit that needs feeding, anything is better than the rhythm of everyday life and the bondage of always knowing what you are going to do next. In my kitchen back home I would watch my middle son peal potatoes for Sunday lunch as my eldest son watched a movie on the TV. My little girl would finger through her brother's books and I would sweep the floor, but in another moment in time I was also in that plane where I saw the edges of a desert shim down from a land God described in the Bible, which turned blood red as the sun dropped to the horizon and the sand lapped at the shores of the Arabian Sea.

As we saw in the distance the dark brooding interior of India I watched the wing flaps begin to extend as we descended. It was easy to see fishermen's night lights off the shores of Maharastra. When the flaps dipped to braking position, Mumbai's streetlamps almost joined the runway until you saw men hunched around sentry fires as we came in to land.

INDIA

The flight to Bahrain was an Airbus 320. At just six seats wide with a central aisle, it was a small plane. The pocket of air around us was smooth and it could not have been an easier journey. Only by riding on this journey would I really know what was possible and what was not, and I was only now finding time to write down what I had seen and done.

In some of the hard journeys in my past I have looked back at what I've done and known that if I would not have been capable of replicating the experience. So hard were some of my cycling journeys that any repeat of unnecessary effort filled me with dread. I would soon realise that this journey was to hold the same fear. The bar had been set at a high level and that linked to the same self-imposed pressure to succeed. Each day was dependent on conditional achievement; that is to say, should I stop reaching the project's goals, the journey as a whole could not be successful – there is a point when the little time you lose each day cannot be made up. You have simply fallen too far behind to stand a chance of rescuing the record. I knew already that this was the last time I would attempt such a circumnavigation by motorcycle. Each day could be my nemesis. If I didn't reach the time and distance that was necessary to win back my record, I knew I would suffer for the rest of my life. This was a position I didn't want to go to as it reminded me of the time when my father died. I missed his actual passing away. His last breath was spent alone and I got to his bedside minutes too late. That instant, I knew, I would not forgive myself and I never have. Journeys can be seen as examples of standards of what you might expect from your life. The 50 heroes who sailed with Jason on the Argo in the quest for the *Golden Fleece* were as one in their commitment to succeed. Argus built the boat and Tiphys and Ancaeus were the pilots. I felt like them as I nailed my every waking hour to the hero's post; it was easier to win the battle than lie ignominiously in defeat.

★ ★ ★ ★ ★

I arrived at Mumbai airport at four in the morning when Aditya collected me in a cab and took me into the city. Jiten had used one of his extensive contacts to have people meet me here and in Calcutta. My instinct to employ Jiten, a young man from Ahmedabad, was inspired. He now lived in Delhi and was a highly intelligent and resourceful guy, which he needed to be with all responsibilities to 'hold the fort' for me back home in Wales. He had taken over the complete coordination of this record ride, which was something I had relied on major sponsors to do for me in the past. If there was a problem, all I had to do was brief him about it and he would be on the phone, arranging, pestering, and in his inimitable and charming way, persuading. The day before the bike was due to be shipped to India we found out that Indian customs were reluctant to transport dangerous goods out of the country. This would have meant not riding there and flying directly from Istanbul to Bangkok, which would reduce the credibility of the project. As mentioned earlier, I had told Jiten to have an Enfield Bullet waiting for me in Mumbai and while my R1 was clearing customs in Istanbul and Bangkok, I would spend three days riding across to Calcutta anyway. Of course, the concept of a *'Circumnavigation of the World by Motorcycle'* allowed only for the use of the same bike throughout, so this part of the journey could not count for Guinness or any other verification authority, but that was not in the spirit of my adventure. For me, India had to be included. It is the hardest continent in the world to motor across. It would be unthinkable in extreme motorcycling terms not to test myself against road life here on this, my sixth circumnavigation of the world.

Aditya was a young chap from Pune who worked for *Overdrive*, the foremost motoring magazine in the country. Through Jiten's friend Shirish, the assistant editor, Aditya was given the job of looking after me until I rode out of the city. A room in their offices was at my disposal and after a quick shower I grabbed a couple of hours of much needed sleep. Late morning I was woken and we went around the corner to one of the trendy all air-con coffee shops that have sprung up in major cities to exploit India's new affluence.

We chatted for a while and apart from my brief conversations with Ikbal and Paolo, the journey from the UK to here had afforded me precious little free time. Boys from the Bullet Club of Mumbai were due to meet me the next day on the Sunday, by which time my bike would have landed and the initial stages of customs clearance begun. I was hopeful I'd be on the road on the Monday and had already decided to leave at the earliest opportunity whatever the time of day or night. The spirit of this adventure was to connect with the bike after custom controls and get back on the road as quickly as reasonably possible. To put it simply, less 'downtime' means more credibility.

We jumped in a cab and I called Jiten and we talked through elements of the project. The bike would be flown out today, Saturday, and the customs clearance would start on the Monday and should be clear by Tuesday. The idea that the clock stopped during these periods when the bike was incarcerated went against my purist concept of riding a bike around the world fast. Dealing with bureaucracy was the canny bit and arguably deserved to be included in the process of any circumnavigation, but the existing rules militated against this. Very rich people could fly in their private jet and by-pass normal custom controls. The system was clearly open to abuse. If you decided to keep the bike in customs for a while longer and take a holiday, you could and the *Guinness Book of Records* in their simple, office-based understanding of such things, found this acceptable. The motorcar record is 19 days, but apparently it took the three drivers nearly six months to get the job finished.

So I slept, and then the next day I woke up much refreshed. Having flown into the city in the early morning, a pattern was being established that every time I found a bed I just slept. It took an hour to get through Indian immigration and another hour to get to my room. I still had no travelling stamina and after the flight from Istanbul I was really tired. Already my dreams were getting more vivid and required the blanket of sleep. This is a phase in a journey that precedes the point when you have to ride night and day. It's a bunker mode which your brain adopts because it doesn't want to face what you are preparing to do. I was slightly in shock, thrown out from my comfortable existence to a harsher place where most of the rest of the world resides, and I just needed a little time to catch up with the ambitious nature of what was about to happen. It is true that depressives sleep a lot, and I wasn't that, but my ability just then, to think coherently was impaired and I just hoped the true capabilities that have taken me around the world so many times before, would kick in. It wasn't that the journey was too hard; the bike riding pushed me to my limit, the technical process of getting around was already tiresome, and the simple biological time clock was starting to unravel, and I also couldn't say yet if there was real meaning to the project. If there was a depression, it was linked to an inability to express certain values I felt this journey represented, even if it was an articulate discussion of how little meaning it had. As

I sunk into sleep I dreamt of fans stirring sweaty air, in turn warming and cooling, the rotary rhythm soothing gently until I dreamt no more.

★ ★ ★ ★ ★

The film star James Caan said that *until the actor loses all sense of self, the character never comes to life* and in the same sense that an actor is transported from self to stage character, this can be one way of dealing with an equally dramatic transition from ordinary life to road life. In method acting, performances are drawn from the actor's own personal experiences and emotions and it refers to not emoting in the traditional manner of stage conventions, but to speak and gesture in a manner used in private life. Marlon Brando in On the Waterfront and Al Pacino in Taxi Driver were both exponents of method acting. Purposefully or unwittingly, travellers often take on the character they feel they need to be in order to survive: polite person, tough person, vulnerable person or in my case, fast person, so you don't get stuck on the side-walk talking to people for too long. It's not a normal stage, it's far more intense than that; it's a real drama with life and death issues. The philosopher Aristotle theorised that tragedy results in an emotional cleansing for the audience and that this explains why people like seeing dramatised pain. Unlike the way a playwright can plot, there didn't seem, for me, to be the luxury of any surprise intervention by any unseen factors that might change the outcome of my event. There was no chance of a *deus ex machina*, a 'God from a Machine' intervening on my behalf to save me. It was, successfully or otherwise, all down to me. Every twist of my head to see, each counter-steer, a sixth sense in traffic, each lean into every corner was a precise movement which if I didn't do correctly meant I might die. In the way that modern writers of tragedy have been known to dispute the conventional view of the genre – criticized for not having any deaths – I too consistently tried to eliminate all events that could overshadow the successful conclusion of all the epic journeys in my life, to ensure that somehow, I too, didn't die.

★ ★ ★ ★ ★

In the early years of travelling it can be hard to be yourself, but after a while you learn to relax into a style of movement that suits your approach to journeying. Travelling slowly allows you to hide away from a backdrop of people and places. Travelling quickly makes you very visible but no sooner are you in the neighbourhood, then you are gone. My style was to journey quickly, to absorb other people's emotions immediately and give back the same. Sceptics would question the notion of your spirit being debilitated by people who want to suck you dry, breathe you in. Rationalists would offer the view that once the other character realises a depth of feeling can be handled, they tell you about those deep things which are normally kept secret. They are the closet stories; the skeletons in the cupboard; secrets which you take in small parcels as you pass quickly by. Sometimes you are in the most superficial of circumstances hearing the deepest of human feelings. These people see you as a safe vessel in which huge emotions can be deposited; laying them to rest as if whispering to a sacred tree.

Emotional overload has to rest on wide shoulders and an *alter ego* can provide a wider platform on which this can sit. A trusted friend, so close that he is almost part of you. For me, he was called *The Interviewer* because I needed to find out what this journey meant and whether *meaning* was part of the process. It was too easy to stay in the comfort zone. To say *'because it is there,'* meant nothing to me. We all know it's *there*, whatever *it* is. Why adventurers / round the world bikers / yachters / mountaineers and the like do what they do is interesting if tagged with any search for the *meaning of life*, but how to frame it? I made a few notes such as in a novel, where you create subject matter such as, 'man tries to find meaning in his life'; plot includes journeys to the other side of the planet; add characterisation – self plus alter ego; include cast of thousands; enhance storyline; re-address subject; debate what constitutes *meaning,* give it intellectual identity, create a voice and position it where you think it needs to be heard.

★　★　★　★　★

In the Café Mondegar near the Regal Cinema on the Colaba Causeway downtown, The Doors and Pink Floyd played to a young clientele. Next to the juke box I sat quietly drinking a coffee. Most sat around small square tables, drinking, some smoking, chatting, occasionally hugging and kissing in (for India) an uncharacteristically and expressive modern way. This was one of the cool places in Mumbai where hip youngsters hung out, travellers arranged to meet, but what it really represented was the upturn in the fortunes of the city. When I first visited Mumbai it was a beautiful and architecturally superior city, but for ordinary people, distinctly apart from the rich middle classes, it had a grey and industrial outlook. In India, modern guilt-free fun time has only just begun to percolate down the socio-economic order. This is due to improved economic wealth, but two of the three most common elements in the universe are hydrogen and stupidity.

"Ah, this is an interesting if not obscure point you are making."

"What! About stupidity?" I looked around and saw no one actually talking to me, "I'm not even sure it was a point, I just said it, and where are you?"

"You'll not find me because I'm in your head. I'm your alter ego for this journey. How do you do?" Suddenly, I was kind of talking to myself, or rather I wasn't, it was more like thinking out loud. *'Oh my God I'm a weirdo!'* yet it didn't feel weird. All my childhood I had watched my Dad talk to himself as we walked over the hills together. He would tell me little stories about his life, ordinary stories made bigger by time. He would then drift for a while and then describe conversations he'd had with his father and sometimes he'd just describe exactly what he was doing just then, to himself. The Australian aborigines call it 'dream walking' and they talk their poems and dream words as they trek along their song lines. And when they did, their children would be strapped to mama's back and as the child felt each footfall and heard the crunch of the soil mix with the words, the land and voice would become one and the same, mental signposts indicating their way across the wilderness.

"One day there will be an unchanging state where all the molecular particles in the world and the universe will have broken down to their constituent parts; protons, electrons, anti-matter, quarks; everything will be at absolute zero; no life, no light, no change for ever. This is what your future is," said the Interviewer in my head.

"What, you still here? I mean, great!" I said sardonically, "no motorbikes, no women, no cinemas!"

"Nothing. Forget your sex life and your hobbies,"

"What sex life?" I said.

"Look, be serious, the facts are, that we are finite creatures thrown onto an unremarkable planet in an unremarkable galaxy, bequeathed with an inheritance of genes, a product of forces which we dimly understand and over which we have no control."

"Doesn't sound very promising,"

"It isn't. Everything will end and everything we do has questionable meaning."

"So what's the point of doing things like motorcycling around the world?"

"There isn't any point. You think it beats the meaningless of replication; going to work, shuffling through stuff that you think gives you meaning? Look at you huh, you do the same ordinary things as anyone else – jump on planes, hang about, wait for the bike to arrive, drink coffee, ride loads of miles, see things in a blur, nil conversations, jump on more planes, eat, drink, hang around. Isn't this the same?"

"Not everyone goes around the world," I said meekly,

"Take out the planes and the bikes and what have you got?"

"Drink coffee, see things in a blur?"

"Hardly the song-lines you describe?"

"I never feel the earth beneath my feet."

"Precisely."

★ ★ ★ ★ ★

Enforced by the State Governments policy in their CNG cleaner fuel policy for public transport, Mumbai was cleaner than ever before. Historically, like all Indian cities, belching fumes created a Victorian smog of carcinogens that sat in the air like some Brownian motion. One day in 1992 I rode from Jaipur to Mumbai as part of my Enfield world tour and arrived smothered in soot. My face was black and my brain was laced with diesel which rather detracted from the view that travel is good for the mind. In a literal sense it has probably shortened my life and any minute I expect to collapse from an embolism having breathed in too many mutant particles from the exhausts of smoky trucks. Yet death is a small price to pay for a life that is bonded with mythology. There is more than a link with the James Dean experience of 'burn brightly, die young' than I had ever dared connect with me. After all, I was an ordinary man with no film star status and would just simmer and live a long life, unlike Dean, who had money, looks, celebrity credibility and still he found no meaning in his life. It is the ordinary ones who have to carry on, pay the bills, hold together family life, get a decent haircut or make sense of a senseless situation.

One cold beer later and I felt more forgiving and called a cab to make our way back along the causeway. Across the bay a big red sun sank behind Malabar Hill where the film stars, models and the politicians live, and is home to some of the costliest pieces of real estate in the world. In Indian cities, when the cab driver stops at lights, to save fuel he switches off his engine. Then, for a few brief moments, everything goes quiet. A landscape of people move but in the way the sound of a bike coming towards you is different to it going away, the change in sound here made everyone look slow.

"You see the idea of meaning is something philosophers have debated since the onset of self consciousness."

"You're arrogant to think you have any answers, I mean you're only an average kind of intelligence and you're trying to be smart."

"Questioning and trying to find answers is a perfectly acceptable way of dealing with your limitations and your ignorance."

"Ok," I said, "I'm listening, but if people somehow give themselves meaning isn't that what it's all about?"

"OK, but you need to go back to the beginning to understand meaning. At the onset of life on earth, you had the primordial soup, then, creatures responded only to fundamental stimuli; light, heat, water currents and the like. After millions of years of evolution they became conscious, like a dog, for example, and then eventually self consciousness evolves, as with humans who begin to examine themselves almost as a separate entity."

Suddenly the cab shuddered into life and we lurched forward to do battle with metal and flesh. On the way back to where I was staying for the night I started to feel tired. I'd had no sleep on the plane and had had only six hours sleep in 144 hours. It didn't seem possible but it was true. After getting back to the room I lay on the bed with the light on almost afraid to go to sleep thinking I'd never wake. After a couple of hours, Aditya knocked on my door and I shot upright still asleep until I mumbled something and realised where I was. The quicker you travel, the more your sense of orientation becomes confused. In order to know what direction you need to go, looking at the position of the sun is a worthy but wasted opportunity and whilst a chap in Mumbai tried to sell me a sextant, even the position of the stars would be lost on me. Anyhow, I didn't need constellations to find somewhere to eat and we went downstairs to send photos back to Jiten in Wales, then we hopped on Aditya's bike and went out for dinner.

As a rule, when I wasn't sleeping I was riding; when not riding, I was filming and in between all this, I was writing. Just occasionally I looked up from the basement and found a world waiting to be enjoyed as opposed to being merely recorded.

★ ★ ★ ★ ★

There was a film I related to called 'The Truman Show', which Jim Carrey starred in. All the elements surrounding his life were literally a complex film set. Truman Burbank lives happily in a small, peaceful and beautiful town called Seahaven. He has a good job, a nice wife, and basically a happy life, until he starts to suspect that his life is a fake. The town of Seahaven is really an extremely big film studio (the Great Wall of China and the Truman Show studio-dome are the only things that can be seen from space). The town is full of cameras, in which the world's most famous reality show, The Truman Show is recorded and broadcast to the entire world. The main character, Carrey playing Truman, doesn't know this or that everyone in the town is an actor. I had begun to record everything about my life and suddenly I felt the parallels with The Truman Show, except that I hadn't yet realised how much of my life was part of my own imagination and how much was real.

★ ★ ★ ★ ★

The next day was Sunday and I had time off. The freighting agent's office was closed until Monday morning and the bike would be arriving only late evening on Gulf Air. I felt a bit lonely and wondered who waited for the Argonauts, for their return home? Who waited for the helmsman? Exactly who were the partners of the great travellers of history? How did Mrs Polo stick it out with her husband when he spent so much time in the company of Mr Khan? Unanswerable, so I hauled myself out of bed, showered, dressed and went around the corner with my long-suffering companion Aditya to a small restaurant for breakfast. We ate a pureed dish of Pao-Bhaji, a Gujarati fusion dish consisting of potatoes, tomatoes, capsicum, onions and French beans mopped up with a bread bun and all washed down with piping hot tea. After this we walked a little further and into a modern café and enjoyed a European cappuccino. He sat quietly as I wrote my diary and responded to texts on my mobile phone. The loneliness of the long distance traveller is severe and sometimes he has to resist the temptation of running into the arms of the first person to show him kindness. They all did that, the mythological characters, fell in love with their Gods and Goddesses. Throughout history conquerors and explorers have been tested by the moments when they have had to confront the darkness alone.

Two weeks into the trip, miles away from any successful conclusion, an age away from making any sense, I felt it was beginning to take on a different meaning. The fact that I had more time allowed me to think. Riding a bike for 24 hours a day prevented me from indulging in any philosophical thought. A million items of road furniture each day fractured my thinking and reduced me to appreciate a little more how the gyroscopic effect of moving forward was the only thing that kept me upright. In between the punishment of fast riding and having to ratchet my thoughts into order, somewhere, somehow, this journey had to have meaning and increasingly this was becoming important for me to try to resolve.

"Did you know about the Cicada that lie buried for 17 years?" my *alter ego* interviewer suddenly said to me. I was scratching my head wondering why I was thinking like this. It was 17.33 Indian time, 12.33 in London and 4.33am on the west coast of America. I was more concerned about a conversation I'd just had with my children. The boys were missing me badly and cleverly formulated questions to keep me on the line, whilst my daughter was beginning also to get the hang of how to capture daddy's attention. Willow, being older, grasped the nettle and understood perfectly that India was way beyond Europe and nowhere near America. Juno had no idea about India except that he knew Jiten was from Delhi and worked with Dad and Tatyana just wanted me to bring back a Barbie doll on my motorbike. *"Focus, the cicada!"*

"What about it? What relevance has this idea got to me?"

"Meaningfulness."

"What?"

"We are talking about the meaning of things or how things might be perceived as being meaningless. Some things that might appear meaningful, say, like us having to get an important report discussing y to x on time begs the question of it necessarily being meaningful. All you are going to do is pass on this technical process to your children so they possibly do the same thing."

"This is an obvious old chestnut, but we all have to do this kind of stuff,"

"Yes, but it isn't biologically meaningful – it's been created to support a political / social system which we only partly understand and have no control over." There was a pause. "So what do you think about the cicadas?"

"What?" I said.

"The cicadas live for 17 years and almost all of this time is spent underground."

"Why?"

"It thins out the predators."

I didn't see the connection.

"This insect burrows for all of its life, briefly erupts for a nuptial flight to reproduce, lays its eggs and in a few days it dies. The eggs hatch and the progeny do likewise and burrow underground for the next 17 years. You see, by staying out of reach of its predators, it permits a greater chance of survival. Unless, as a predator, you equip yourself with a method to withstand such a famine you are going to die out."

"And how does this relate to motorcycling?"

"Wait. When the new generation fly they do so in great profusion, mate, and a massive new generation allows for the tremendously successful continuation of the species. This is meaningless if you look at the lifestyle, but not if you're counting numbers. The general lack of consciousness involved makes it impossible for this to be absurd. If you look deeply at everything, there is a combination of meaning, meaninglessness and absurdity. You motorcycling around the world in say, 18 days, is meaningful to you, meaningless to someone who would do it in three or four years. If, as a conscious rider, you are aware that it somehow lacks meaning to go so far so quickly, it becomes absurd."

"I'm really confused. But I disagree because this journey really does have purpose, it earns money and pays the bills."

"So does going to the office. Riding so many miles or filing so *much paperwork is equally repetitive, so QED — the same dilemma has to be overcome."*

"I struggle myself with the meaning of this journey but it could be seen to be maybe original, brave and tenacious, but not absurd."

"The philosophical definition of absurdity requires comprehension of meaninglessness. The real soup of understanding lies between the seriousness we give our lives, the harsh reality of our needs, fiscal and otherwise, the conservative nature of our goals and the meaninglessness that absolutely everyone has to suffer from time to time. The more you realise what your project lacks, the more absurd it becomes when you continue to persevere with it."

"We are discussing the meaning of life here, and that is a question, which we can all discuss but have no answers. Brighter brains than me have concluded only the most esoteric values and mathematicians write it out using formulae so what chance have I got?"

"That's not what we are discussing, whether you have any answers, of course you don't, what is interesting is that we are discussing it." In a sense that was right. A computer technician can no longer build a computer from scratch, but buys individual components: the motherboard, items of circuitry, hard drives and Random Accessed Memory in the way that all of us are mostly assemblers, increasingly part of someone else's intellectual shrubbery. At that I went to bed, slept badly, got up to the sound of market traders erecting their stalls and started to wander about, because that's what you do when you travel.

★ ★ ★ ★ ★

All things can be viewed in different ways and the meaning changes depending on this view. Sitting in my room reading the *Times of India* I read a report by Mr Vishal Sharma openly discussing the cartographical discrepancy between Cartesian and Arno Peters' Projection. Open a child's geography book and Greenland and Scandinavia appear to be 10 and three times larger than India respectively. Actually, Greenland is only 80% of India's size and Scandinavia three times smaller. Russia appears bigger than the entire continent of Africa, Alaska larger than Mexico and tiny Europe is larger than the whole of the South American continent! According to Mr Sharma, this Mercator map was made during the age when Europe dominated and exploited the world – the homelands of the white rulers are portrayed to be large and non-white countries small. This was all made to artificially portray the territorial superiority of the colonial powers, and to make a psychological impression of this sense of power over what was perceived as a less strong mindset. Planet Earth is a tri-axial ellipsoid, moving around the Sun in an elliptical orbit at 30 kilometres per hour, rotating around it's axis at 1666 kilometres per hour which is faster than the speed of sound. Such high speed rotation has resulted in the polar areas being compressed towards the centre and the equatorial areas being bulged out, thus explaining why the Earth is not a perfect sphere. The difficulty in representing three dimensional spherical geometry into a two dimensional Cartesian one relies on trying to apply one mathematical model from one particular paradigm to another when, according to Mr Sharma, it clearly cannot work.

In 1974, the United Nations acknowledged this map-making discrepancy and accepted a new map made by the German Arno Peters and called it the Peters' Projection. I've known about this for a while and knew it had equal areas and equal representation of all the land and sea surfaces of the world. Peters' map is based on a decimal grid which divides the surface of the Earth into a hundred longitudinal fields of equal width and a hundred latitudinal fields of equal height. It treats the rectangles around the equator as equal squares and builds the other rectangles onto these proportions to the area they represent. The grid marked on the map is itself based on the traditional 180 degrees and all North-South lines run vertically. Geographical points can be seen in their precise directional relationship. The East-West lines run horizontally. The Peters' map therefore shows all areas whether countries, continents or oceans according to their actual size. For any overland circumnavigation a true scale of the endeavour can be much better understood. To motorcycle across India using the Cartesian model cannot compare to the one created by Arno Peters and puts such a journey into perspective. All the more reason why India cannot be left out of such a journey when antipodal references have also to be built into the consensus about exactly what constitutes a journey *'around the world'*. That's why I have stuck with India.

* * * * *

Bruce and the Bullet boys from Mumbai call themselves *The Indie Thumpers* and they came to collect me at my place in Dadar, a suburb 20 minutes north of Mumbai city centre. We then set off south, once again to have a few beers. I didn't know quite why we were all together but there is often a distinct commonality and understanding between bikers, wherever you are. We went to the sea and took some photos and then headed back to Café Mondegar not far from the Gateway of India. We chatted over Kingfisher beers and listened once again to the retro music – Dire Straits and The Doors. As usual I was trying to write in my journal about the essence of travel and how it was linked to searching. The problem about travel is that you don't know what you are searching for. You rummage forward more blind than a mole and with the hearing of a deaf man and slowly, more than slowly, at a speed that hardly moves, you begin to understand how the concept of gained knowledge can be at the same time exciting but also a hapless, fraudulent task; for as soon as you learn something, that knowledge extends like some ever-growing tentacle, and you have as many corridors as there are fish in the sea, down which you are certain to get lost.

From near the Gateway of India we jumped on the bikes and rode almost the length of the city, bottom to top, to eat food in an open air stall in Mahim. The Kathi-Kebabs and Chicken Spring Rolls were excellent whilst the Bheja Fry more suspect when I realised that it's goat's brains sandwiched and pressed between fried bread. This area is the second most sensitive in the city due to it having a predominantly Muslim population. If anything kicks off, this is one of the places it starts. The food was freshly cooked and hot and the Bullet boys were great company. They were all off to Ladakh later in the month and given their travel and financial restrictions, they were all adventurers riding as well as they could.

That night I dreamt of home. I slept soundly and I dreamt of my children. Our concept of time was similar – both based on the elastic nature of time and distance. My youngest boy would ask me where I was and if I was going to come home tomorrow, and my oldest boy's only concern was whether I would see any elephants. What I did had little real meaning to them, and only so much to me, which was pathetic, and chiding myself, I woke as Aditya knocked on my door to warn me we should go and see the freighters. But the questioning in my head remained for the rest of the day like some sort of residual, emotional, déjà vu.

Anything was better than dealing with Indian paperwork, even nostalgia. As we sat in the cab on the Express Highway somewhere near the airport I was taken back to the last time I'd imported a bike here. From a logistical point of view it made no sense because India didn't need to be incorporated into the schedule. It was a view I held that the journey would have more credibility if it included a greater variety of motoring experience. Many years ago my Dad asked me which path I was going to choose to run my life, the easy way or the hard way, and I replied that I would take the hard way, and in hindsight, what a bloodied nose of a way it has been.

At the freighting agents' office Mr Prakash told me that the bike was in the country and that I should go directly to the Indian Automobile Association in Churchgate, centrally located in downtown Mumbai and from there, have the RAC in Bristol fax them to confirm that the Carnet documents relating to the bike were genuine. That would then be passed onto Customs and 24 hours later the bike should be released. Leaving Mumbai early evening is not such a bad thing as I would have the coolness of two nights and only one hot day to reach Calcutta. Should I overrun, then I would be arriving in the morning of the second day with a prospective average mileage of 350 miles per 12 hour period. Already I have improved my 1997 ride by two days in Europe and it looks as if I might gain two days in India. That will be down to a 28 day schedule compared to my 31 day '97 solo record, but still at least a day longer than the existing pillion record.

So we jumped into another cab to the West Indian Automobile Association and stopped for a coffee in the Mocha Café just down the road in Churchgate, also famous for the railway station that sends the Up Train to Delhi and the Down Train to Chennai (formerly Madras). It was vital I got the RAC to fax me confirmation of the integrity of the Carnet and then I realised it was a public holiday in England. This has happened to me before and it meant another day hanging about as I was powerless to move the project on. Secretly I didn't mind, apart from the rest, but simply because I could take in more of the smells of India. The sidewalk supported a crusty odour best described as unwashed. The monsoon was due to start in a couple of weeks and that would change things. A smell of cool spring would last briefly until swamped by rising sewers. Whilst I was entering India at the hottest point in her season it was still preferable to the rains.

The record-breaking nature of this project singled it out for funding and sponsorship. It was definitely not a holiday. There was no structure that allowed for the collection of souvenirs other than mental ones. The moment I decided to introduce India into the route I knew it would be a headache, but a charming one at that. After aborting our mission to establish my right to rush the bike through customs we walked around, first to a bookshop, then for a *chai*, which is Indian tea. Across the road I bought some Bani-Buri, which consisted of a finely crafted wheat flower cup with a small hole finger punched in the top to accommodate a little mashed Chana Dal, reminiscent of yellow corn; to this was added sweet tamarind water followed by another water made of chilli paste, chilli powder, rock salt and other common spices. This was followed by yet more chai; at two and half rupees it's the Asian sub-continent's best value gift to the world. No one makes tea like the Indians. The main ingredient, tea leaves, are diffused with cardomen and ginger. Chai of course differs between regions. In Kashmir for example, Kehwa chai consists of tea leaves grown in Afghanistan, brewed in plain water and then once strained, almonds are added along with cardomen and sugar to taste. Chai would differ as I journeyed across India and as this would be my main source of liquid other than bottled water, I was looking forward to the experience.

We walked across the busy road junction, a crossing not

unlike ten thousand others I would weave through on my way to Calcutta. There I bought a couple of glasses of sugar beet juice, squeezed through a mangle. Over the way, a green common ground known as The Oval separated us from the Central Telegraph Office. For many years, and long before STD, ISO cabins and mobile phones, this was the place from which travellers booked telephone calls home. It was from here too that I would speak to my Dad, telling him how I had journeyed on elegant sounding steam locos like the Rajasthan Express or the Hindustani. For his part he would tell me which pub he was going to for his lunchtime pint. When he asked if it was easy to get a ticket, we would discuss the intricacies of the Indian tourist quota system which always meant there would be a berth. It used to take two days and nights to cross the country. I didn't know it then, but having hot desert winds from the Deccan Plateau or the Central Plains dry my body to a parched leaf was part of my training for this journey. For his part, my dad always ended our conversations with a little 'parable', and they were better after the beer than before. He once said, "Remember what Aristotle said, "Builders become so by building and harp players become so simply by playing the harp'. You are an adventurer son because you do adventures, so go and adventure. Do your own thing but for God's sake come back safely to me." I acknowledged him with almost comic reverence, but as time has passed by, I have learnt to bow my head in the face of his humility. He was as astute as he was accurate. Partly because he fathered me, but mostly because he took interest in how I grew, he knew my every thought. When any parents produce a child they give the world the potential for great things to be achieved, but that potential is rarely realised. Having drawn from a life that has been lived in quiet detail, with the simplest of illustrations my dad taught me that my whole world and everything I did, I did for him. Only when you are older does this relationship become clear and as I presented the conclusion of my adventures to him with trepidation, he in return presented me with his views. He taught me to think more specifically about the home of the human condition – which is surely one of the commonalities of conversation when one travels – over and above the tedium of asking each other where we had journeyed from and to. "The greatest physicists in the world agree that we live on a minor planet of a very average star situated on the edge of a hundred thousand million galaxies," he would say to me; and so as to absolve myself of aimlessness in my adventures, marred only by too much innocence or guilt, I created the controlled act of riding a motorcycle as fast as I could; faster than the wind across continents, faster than the thoughts it takes to know why, and from time to time I would land amidst fields with strange foods and people with smiles but always with points of great accuracy.

"Is it of any worth, what I do?" I asked him, and he shook his head and from the perspective of the lowest common denominator he was right. If I had asked him how it, or any small action might affect the world, he would have been equally dismissive, but from the way a butterfly's wing can tamper with a tempest, he was quite out of his depth, and quite wrong.

Why on earth would someone keep on riding around the world like this? Well, to tell a secret, such repetition had become my only contribution to life. The act of motorcycling around the world is such a bizarre and little-known skill – its use to humanity could be described as nil but I was unsure about this. It certainly represented the story of a human being living on the edge; one who crossed ten thousand traffic junctions when it needed only one miscreant with a bullock cart to end it all; when rider, dreamer, essayist and father could, in an instant, have his face forced through skin and bone against the animal's rib cage. Wherever he was in that envelope of space, he had to acknowledge that his life was now just a game of numbers.

The next day I presented myself to the Western Indian Automobile Association and filled in more paperwork. The letter of validation from the RAC to the WIAA couldn't be obtained because the fax machine here reported various code errors but nothing that said it operated correctly. Fortunately Mr Mehta, the grey-haired and kindly chairman took me for coffee and toast and dismissed the need and gave me their letter validating the carnet. This was an important stage prior to the bike being allowed out of customs. This procedure would be in the hands of my freighting agent Mr Prakash who assured me I would be on my way within 24 hours. Of course he couldn't know that for sure. This is what freighting agents do because they have no power. Anybody without power tells you what you want to hear. He wanted to help but he was helpless. Rested, I visualised how it would be to cross India. I cherished the thought of riding through the Indian night and the next day and night and part of the day after that. I wasn't going to stop. Nothing would prevent me from driving through the desert and then the jungle night until, with some small sense of victory, I would reach a soft sweet cool Indian dawn. A little later the sun would rise and burn and later still the sea breeze that would have long since died would be replaced by a humidity in which you could swim. Later still, the heat would be crushing and in my helmet the sweat would start to pour until the salt would sting and make sores around my eyes. By mid afternoon the blood would have drained from my face until, when all the wind had gone, my wrists and feet would blister. As the sun began to set, the day's ride would start to cross into the night and all through this the bike would need to beat perfectly in tune. My ears would have strained all the time for sounds that strike fear into a motorcyclist far from home: something not quite right; an unbalanced valve; something not seated quite right; a choking, perhaps a harshness in the way she purred. Then finally, I would reach the Howrah Bridge in Calcutta. Things at home were not great and if this was all I was Master of, then at least I was Master of something. In a sense I was simply the Commander of my own calling, driven by destiny and like a dog with that bone, both were inseparable.

I walked around to the Mocha Café and made this one of my world stops; a place I would frequent when next in town. For me there would always be another time when I would be here, always on the road to somewhere else. Like a drug it grips you, the make-believe story that you call your life. Sipping coffee, I sat quietly away from the crowds. It was not easy to think about home and the things that had been left behind. There were the small things of no consequence and there where the thoughts of my children. Laughing and playing in my head, I squeezed them tight, praying silently that this journey would keep us all safe. I thought of my friends hoping they were thinking of me and that was my last thought before I stepped back onto the street.

In Mumbai. 1st June 2005

I'll be glad to move on and am looking forward to riding across India. It's always like this, having to deal with the paperwork. It was unfortunate arriving on a weekend and then hitting a Bank Holiday in the UK but I'll be away soon riding through the night. I have no intention of resting but will ride absolutely non-stop for the 1350 miles from Mumbai to Calcutta via Hyderabad. My Indian sources tell me that Mumbai to Calcutta via Delhi means going through Bihar - the poorest and most dangerous state in India and that is definitely out. Mumbai via Nagpur means riding on a recently surfaced road which, by all accounts, has been done badly so we've decided on Hyderabad.

After a few hours I climbed aboard a cab once more and rattled from the Gateway of India past Victoria Terminus to the Causeway, from where I remembered the direction of my lodgings. By the time he'd turned right, away from Malabar Hill, I was asleep. Deep down I was troubled and wanted to hide away; at such times sleep is your only companion. I was stuck in Mumbai and while it was an understandable delay, it was of nightmarish proportions compared to the schedule I'd wanted to keep to. That night I slept badly. The next morning I felt very alone. On the front page of an old Times of India I caught sight of its *'Saying for the Day'*. Quoting an old Persian proverb it said, *'I wept because I had no shoes until I saw a man who had no feet.'* I don't know if this was supposed to make the population of India feel better but it did nothing for me. I got up early, looked at myself in the mirror and saw a man doing what he has done for many years, but older. I looked deeply into this man's eyes and wondered what wisdom, if any, had been etched on to the retinas that would feed directly to his brain. It seemed that as this man blinked, he was simply a man, like all men, who saw desperate ambition alongside a realisation that he would probably never get to where he wanted to be. He brushed his teeth. When he closed his eyes and opened them again to see if he was still there, he was. The 18th century philosopher Bishop Berkeley famously maintained that when you close your eyes it's only because God keeps looking at you that you continue to exist. When this 21st century man reopened his eyes and looked closer, the lines on his face seemed to be saying that with so many miles and stories etched into his visage from ear to ear, it would be obscene to let him die just yet when there was still so much to be done. He smiled and agreed. 'Fairly fine job so far you funny looking bastard!' he said to himself and carried on with his day.

★ ★ ★ ★ ★

Immediately I went downstairs, drank a chai and jumped into the same cab with the same driver as yesterday. My white trousers were less white but clean and the tee-shirt I was wearing was clean smelling. Fresh in spirit with my newspaper under my arm, we bumped along past the billboards and the thousands of small businesses, which, with their incessant industriousness, made this one of the busiest and most populated places on earth. Insulated from my immediate environment, I looked out through the cab window at the beggars and the severely crippled. They were still there, the terribly dispossessed, except that when the cab stopped at traffic lights small hands managed to catch up with you and touch you on the shoulder and arm. One man had no shoes, in fact he didn't have any feet; so it seems the Times of India's *'saying of the day'* was not just a metaphor. Actually, he didn't have any legs either; he pushed himself along on a trolley using his hands; his torso was strapped hard down so he couldn't fall off. I was reminded of that other saying, "in the land of the blind, the one-eyed man is King'.

Out here in the real world the human condition is neither idealised nor denigrated, it just is. Over the years I and my bikes and my journeys have been touched by the slim wrists of boys and girls who, through hunger, beatings, abuse or illness are now dead. Sometimes there are moments when you feel you don't want to take any more; at those times I tried to imagine what it must have been like for those poor unfortunate kids to get my own troubles back into perspective.

Mumbai's body odour has the whiff of biscuit making in the air, along with dishes on the street such as pav bhaji, all mixed with vegetables and grease stirred in a hot pan. When I took a cab to the freighting agents, handed over the original copy of the letter from the WIAA and returned, I crossed Mahim Creek, a small estuary in sight of the sea and a few hundred yards from Bandra station. The water and mud at low tide was as black as tar and the stench was of unrefined sewage. Surely nothing could survive in these waters, polluted almost beyond imagination? And yet people did. Hundreds of makeshift slum dwellings sat hunched between the road and the water's edge, sticky in the stink.

After dealing with more paperwork I had inched forward the possibility that any moment I would once again be able to ride. I took the same cab home and bought a coffee in a trendy café close to where I was staying. Next door, people crowded round a fight which had just started. The rains had stopped and in a couple of hours I would call my agent Prakash to see if customs were willing to discharge the bike today. I was still hoping to start that night. Then my phone rang, "Mr Nick," said Prakash, from Expeditors, "please come, we need four passport photographs and you have to sign more forms." So I jumped into another cab and met Prakash in Anderhi, a suburb in northern Mumbai by the airport. Once I got my pass into the cargo terminal, I signed the forms, hung around and drank tea. Being here was becoming normal, so much so that I relaxed a little too much and seconds later someone stole my phone. When I called it, the ring tone was engaged, suggesting that someone was calling 'uncle' in Bahrain until Jiten contacted my phone company and disconnected the thief from his international conversation.

'So, Mister Nick, how is it going so far?' said the Interviewer. 'Well my missus has left me and my phone has been pinched and my in-laws don't even know where I am,' I paused, 'I'm sorry, that's family stuff, 'erm I'm fine, it's going well.'

'And Mister Nick,' said the Interviewer, *'tell us what it's like being an adventurer?'*

'Not always great mate,' I said, 'except the bike is taking forever to get out of cargo and here I am flying the bloody flag for India. I didn't have to be here,' I looked around at the street, 'but I love the place so much I wanted to be here. I love India,' and I said this emphatically, 'and I love Indians, but they take forever at customs and they *tea-leaf* telephones.' After which I drank up and went to bed.

When I got back Aditya and I spent some time sending emails. Now I had no phone at least I wasn't going to be distracted by text messages, *'Go-Nick-Go'*, was a common well-meaning message which cost me two dollars to receive. Right now it was not certain I'd get anywhere at all. Much of my time was spent waiting in the wings for my curtain call. And in any case, if I mentioned 'Hyderabad' for example, which of my friends even knew which state this fine city was in, let alone anything else about it? After sending out a few more emails we went to the local bottle shop and downed some Kingfisher beer disconsolately. I called my mate Matt in Delhi, who talked me out of riding to Calcutta via Nepal. He said that there were too many road blocks and the Maoists might confiscate my bike for the war effort. I bet they would, but they'd probably die on the first corner, not being used to 178 brake horse power.

I imagined the scenario:

'This very fast bike' said the Maoist guerrilla on my R1, *'Confucious say too much horse power bad for brain.'*

'You're smoking too much,' said I, 'you're better off sticking with your Enfield'.

'Ah Enfield!' he said, his eyes lighting up.

'Yea, blat blat blat on a nice little Enfield, *ooer* here comes a corner, plenty of time to brake, time for a cup of tea!'

The beer was talking and it talked me in and then out of going to Kathmandu. Matt was right, the little gits would pinch my R1, chuck it down a hillside and use it for a road block.

'So Mister Nick,' the Mumbai Interviewer continued, *'what do you think of it all so far?'*

'You again! Complete bollocks mate. So much for riding around the world. It was easier nine years ago, less paperwork. Also, I've been away for a week and still only done 76 hours of riding because I'm stuck in bloody Mumbai. Don't get me wrong, I'd like to bring the family, but my present mission is a little different'.

'Ah yes'.

'Ah friggin' no'. I was cross. Not with India, nor Mumbai, neither was I pissed off with the air freighters or the nice men in customs shovelling their paperwork from desk to bin and back. No, I was peeved with myself, with my own ridiculous levels of loyalty. I so wanted to come to India and prove how it could be integrated into a round-the-world project. I was kind of cross with my own high level of ambition. Was this journey really necessary? And if it was, I was angry that motorcycling projects like this didn't get the attention they deserved; annoyed with mountaineers, sailors, complete idiots who walked to the North Pole and anyone who thought they were better than everyone else when it was obvious they were considerably more stupid.

Tomorrow would be different. After today I would be in a better mood and become a bike rider again and start a dignified odyssey across the Indian sub-continent. Tomorrow is the beginning of the rest of this ride when the first R1 ever to tread this soil would be fired up in anger. If my instinct could be trusted, it was probable that the experience would be something special, otherwise what would be the point of being here? All any biker wanted was to ride, but my head was starting to shout. Enough waiting for customs! Enough sneering from people who didn't think this project could be accomplished! Enough disrespect from someone who was sailing in a Sargasso Sea with a man who didn't know how to paddle! Enough was enough. I had nothing, absolutely nothing else to say, apart from enough!

The next morning I was licking my wounds. Much improved in temperament but I still couldn't get out of bed. The previous evening I had raised the roof with my freighting agents and informed them how much they reminded me of other incompetent fools I'd also known in the past. I immediately bit my tongue and in the cold light of an early morning in Mumbai wished I had been gentler. It just wasn't Prakash's fault or that of his boss Eric. If you push Mumbai customs officials around too much you are frozen out and they keep you waiting for weeks. If I played my hand badly today I might as well pack up and go home. Today was Friday and I had until late afternoon to get the bike released before everything closed down for the weekend again. A cool frame of reference counted for everything in any kind of expedition but I was almost beside myself with frustration. I'd lost my phone, sullied the schedule because of my excessive loyalty to a country I had spent much time in during my youth and as a result I'd seriously jeopardised the credibility of this project. Or had I? Did anyone really take it as seriously as me? A precious few, perhaps. Soon the road miles would clock up impressively, especially as I was going to ride non-stop day and night until either I collapsed or reached the end of each stage. It was hard to keep up the impetus stuck in a hotel room, but great tests come in different guises.

Each morning, the vendors on my street now waved to me. When I walked past the Royal Fast Food shop and the Ayurvedic Spa Centre, the chaps offered their little sideways nod in friendship. Several times I called Prakash, sent emails and controlled my business from here. Back in Wales, Jiten was coordinating everything. It was a strange role reversal for him, being from Delhi and now stuck in a small village in Wales, me in Mumbai. This project could not be allowed to fail. Sponsorship support was conditional on my not failing and I felt that this single journey would either crown or jeopardise my reputation after 25 years of successful adventuring.

I bought my paper from the same vendor and drank my coffee in the same coffee mart. I read in the Times about a young woman from the Punjab climbing Everest. Floundering at 7000 metres, she had teamed up with a guided expedition to take her to the top. It was taking her two hours to crawl along a 50 metre ridge and then two hours to crawl back, terrified to continue and unable to go on. Family prestige keeps her there and all her family do is offer more money thinking that will solve the problem. The leaders of the climb think she will die and the girl accepts that should this happen she will die in peace. As I order one more coffee, Sherpas have been dispatched to her with batteries for her satellite phone so she can make one last call to ask permission from her family to come home.

At last the phone call I'd been waiting for: Prakash gave me the all clear so I grabbed Bert from the office downstairs and we shot off in a cab to the Cargo Complex by the airport. On the way Prakash phoned Bert and said the bike was completely free of all restrictions and to his word, as we approached the main gate, the bike was being wheeled out. It was lovely to see this sexy little girl. I suppose I had subconsciously awarded my bike the status of female because, let's face it, this machine was a seriously hot number and I loved sitting on her. She was fast, saucy in the corners and when I went down on her, clutching at her as we leaned over together I sometimes lost my breath it was so exciting. Immediately I went over to the shippers' office and got changed. They typed out a letter confirming my exact time of departure from customs and when I went back to the bike she was surrounded by admirers. I wasn't wrong, this bike would win over India. The YZF R1 is the equivalent of Miss World, completely useless in a third world country, but a pleasure to have between your legs for most of the day.

Leaving Mumbai 3rd June 2005

Just had the call from customs that the bike is to be released at around six this evening. I am relieved to say the least. I took a gamble by including India in the schedule because I know what the country has to offer in terms of challenging road riding but also in terms of scenery and the warmth of the people. Any journey across India is amongst the hardest in the world and is undoubtedly dangerous. In my experience riding a bike here is the most dangerous motoring activity in the world. I leave here and head through the night to Pune and on to Hyderabad. I feel good and rested and will aim to complete this second stage in 40 hours. This will mean I am well behind a 1000 mile a day schedule and the pressure will be on to make up time in South East Asia, which I hope to do. I am mindful that if I get through this India stage successfully, then there is a chance I will get the record. At the moment I am very homesick and miss my kids but that is part of what I do. Leaving my family is the hardest part of this adventure. The idea that I can get home quicker is the one thing that keeps me going.

So the journey started across India. After fuelling up and changing money at the international arrival hall of the nearby airport I set off. It had been dark for a while and the rush hour on that Friday night in Mumbai was fierce. It was how I imagine Dickensian London to have been, but with combustion engines instead of horses, carriages and carts. The hustle of the shop-keepers' shouting competed with the fumes and ambient noise, while cars, trucks and mothers with babies all fought for space to get where they needed to go. Men rode their bicycles with briefcases under their arms while vagabonds and murderers, shysters and thieves with daggers up their sleeves all hid in alleyways waiting for their first opportunity to kill you in the dark, or sell you something!

Prising myself through this mayhem didn't take long and soon I was on the Pune Express Highway. This was a six lane carriageway that crossed the Ghats and was forbidden to motorcycles. Of course there were no signs explaining this and when the first toll booth appeared it was expedient to plead ignorance, and as Indians are susceptible to flattery, you simply tell the operators how great India was to have such a fantastic road and naturally they let you through with a nod and a smile. By avoiding the old national highway, I shaved two hours off a very tight schedule. I reached the outskirts of Pune by eleven that evening and everything was on course to cross India non-stop in two days or so. Having stopped for Butter Chicken and three bottles of Thumbs Up, I set off once again for Solapur and aimed not to power nap until around three.

13.37 hours Zaheerabad

The concept of celebrity is upon me. In a sense it's second hand fame because everyone wants to see the bike. Every single time I stop, people start running to me, from across the street, from vendors' stalls. Further back, a near riot ensued. I tried to get a chai (tea) and half the village crowded into the restaurant. As I came out I was jostled and someone punched one of the men and I was told it would be better if I left. After a couple of lassis in a good quality family-run restaurant on the main street of this larger village, there are crowds 15 deep waiting for me to come out. I am quite unused to this and find it a bit intimidating. I wait and rest, hoping they will go away, but why should they go and where? It's their place and if there's one thing an Indian knows little about, it's the idea of privacy. On the other hand, a warm heart and a great smile is normal here.

This was so quick and fast moving it was becoming a simple story about a man on a motorcycle in constant motion and how interesting was that? Well, the motorbike was interesting. She was performing effortlessly, the engine did not miss a beat. The chain was still taut and the take up with gear changes was seamless. The clutch had warmed and the lever was without stiffness, which really applied to every part of the bike. Only the low grade quality fuel caused some limit in performance as she pinked if pushed. The complete lack of hostility made for a predictable ride, which could be construed as uninteresting but my view was that this allowed the rider to focus on the purity of the way the machine interfaced with it's environment. I was more aware of how she reacted to rapid changes in road surface or traffic movement than having to be unduly concerned with mechanical idiosyncrasies.

02:00 hours, on the road in India.
I am about 200 kilometres from Solapur and it's nearly 2 o' clock in the morning. I am riding very well. It's extremely dark, the road is extremely busy and it's a two lane highway and incredibly dangerous. There are trucks everywhere. If I leave a gap in front, obviously an oncoming truck is going to try to overtake and I have to ride over to the left hand side or I'll get hit. If I am riding behind a truck, I am doing 28mph. It's probably the most dangerous road I have ridden in a long time. But India is a great country and I am actually making progress. I'll be in Solapur by 4-5 o' clock in the morning and then I am going to make my way to Hyderabad and I should be there about lunchtime. I'll keep on through the day and then I'll be going onto my next night when I reach the east coast of India and make my way north east to Calcutta.

There was no time to sit and think and the pace that the bike allowed was frightening. At Solapur I cruised through the central part of the city well before it was light and it was quiet. Without the hustle of traffic and people it was easier to see who had homes and who didn't. Unless you are very rich, people who stop moving die very quickly. The bee that stops moving gets swatted and while it may be an unfortunate metaphor for India's poor, you have to admire how quick thinking they need to be to survive. The middle classes also have no room for complacency. They still have to bother to get on the bus and go to work. They have to hang on the outside of trains commuting into Mumbai while the women start preparing dinner on their laps on the way home. The concept of moving to stay alive - or doing something - is critical. Poor people have to sell what they can or beg, moving from car to car carrying a child which might be alive or might be dead, but, they have to move. The poor eventually have to lie down and this was particularly noticeable here as I rode across the centre of Solapur. Hundreds of families lay in heaps like dirty bundles of clothes, asleep on the pavement, sprawled beside the road, against walls, in bus stops, next to rubbish bins, In the morning many of these people would brush themselves down, go to a stand pipe and wash before continuing doing whatever they did before they went to sleep the previous night. Apart from the severity of the poverty, the other harsh quality of a life without money is sheer tedium. As little boys watched their mothers beg, they scratched themselves, pulling off insects or picking at a scab. Perhaps there is a glazed disinterest at both ends of the spectrum; just a thought, but is unlimited choice as emotionally debilitating as having none? Is that boredom on the face of someone who can have anything he wants, or is that my imagination?

Outskirts of Hyderabad Opticians Shop

I had to stop, I was beginning to overheat. I sat by a telephone booth, couldn't talk, heart pounding, core temperature not going down and unlike the bike my own fan hadn't switched on. I sat mostly alone until the usual crowd gathered but I wouldn't answer questions and told everyone to be quiet and not bother me. I was very hot and after ten minutes it began to get better. I called Jiten and left a diary message for the website and then I left. Still needed to cool down so I looked for some air con but found none. Then I went into a posh optician's shop and he had cool, wind-blown air, better than a fan. I sat and I noticed in the mirror that my face was bright red; must be a sign of serious over-heating. No one was bothering me here and very slowly I cooled. Half an hour here was not too much to ask. Temperatures at night didn't drop below 31 degrees centigrade except maybe at the top of the Ghats. I started to make use of my time and wrote my diary entry and drops of sweat were literally hanging on the end of my eye-lashes. My head still hurt but the worst had passed. We were maybe a week, two at the most, from the monsoon and this is the hottest time of the year in India. And I am deep in its interior, in one of the hottest places. No sea breezes. Maybe only Delhi is hotter. When I stop I am surrounded by about a hundred people who almost cut off my air. They make it hard to breathe. In the last town, there were so many people waiting for me to come out I began to realise what it must be like to be famous and I wasn't sure I liked it. It killed what wind there was and made me feel like a small sailing boat in an ocean of people who made my air too hot to breathe.

It took me from late afternoon until it was dark to leave Hyderabad. It looked like an astonishing city but I was not in the best of health and called into a gas station and once again took refuge from the heat. My head was pounding and my face was blood red. The resting that I was doing cooled me only temporarily. I was becoming ill from heat stroke but wasn't recognising the signs. Drinking water wasn't entirely the correct thing to do as it washed away essential electrolytes with nothing being replaced. I was sweating so profusely, my body suddenly stopped operating and couldn't go on. My face looked as if it was going to burst. When I caught sight of myself in the optician's mirror it had the look of someone being destroyed. Yet still it meant nothing. I was sure my body core would cool off and the journey could continue but sunstroke can get steadily worse. Like altitude sickness, you lose sense of what's happening and sometimes cannot correct the process, or don't think you need to. In the gas station I drank some Red Bull but it was weak by comparison to what was needed. Unable to move, my body began to cool a little and I realised that salt replacement and rest was the only cure because my head was throbbing so hard I wanted to hold it in my hands and rock gently from side to side. Outside, the temperature was 43 degrees centigrade and the traffic was jamming up.

16.00 on the 4th June 2005

It's 4 o' clock exactly. I am in Hyderabad . I left Mumbai at about 7:30pm last evening. I've been riding through the night. I think the temperature has touched 45 °C, maybe more … maybe 48 °C. In fact, the lowest temperature last night was 31.5 °C. The road through Maharashtra was very difficult. Trucks were down to 22mph and I was constantly overtaking. Incredibly busy. As I went to Karnataka, the highway improved substantially and I made up some lost ground. I am trying to make 350 miles per 12 hours, which will give me 700 miles every 24 hours. This is about 300 miles down on my 1000 miles a day schedule. It's about 1400 miles from Mumbai to Calcutta. I am not far off the schedule for India and am pleased. I am very exhausted, but it's simply a question of dehydration and I am now drinking properly. The bike has been performing brilliantly, but it's running at 99 degrees centigrade and goes up to 105 – 108 °C as soon as I stop. I am riding better than I ever have and am feeling extremely strong. But also, this is probably the hardest day I have ridden in years. Now I am going to go through the night to Vijaywada and onto the east coast of India and then ride straight through tonight and all day tomorrow to reach Calcutta before midnight on Sunday and straight into customs. I'll fly out to Bangkok on Monday or Tuesday morning at the latest, depending on the flights I get.

Hyderabad is arguably India's fastest growing city and with such a display of western identikit commercialism, it was a credible claim. Leaving the gas station I just managed to climb on the bike and freewheeled onto the road, unable to remember when riding last felt so bad. It was really difficult to ride. Hands swollen, aching all over, I wanted to collapse but what would that serve? Who would look after me then? Why hadn't anyone taught me to look after myself, because this suffering need not have happened. Each journey takes everyone to a place that is hard to get to and harder to get back from. Suddenly, across the road and through the fumes I noticed a chemist and elbowing my way across four lanes of belligerent traffic, I pushed my way inside and pointed to the sun. The chemist knew exactly what was needed and gave me a box of powder. I mixed three sachets in a bottle of coke and carried on. I felt so strange and kneeled down on the ground beside my bike and lay on my back twice more before I left the city limits and already it was dark. I'd got it bad. So far this journey across Hyderabad had taken four hours when it should have taken one. The only reason there was no vomit was because I hadn't eaten anything. Then my nose started to bleed. You can always tell the difference between snot and blood (even if you can't see it) because the loss of blood makes your head feel lighter. Quickly stuffing a piece of newspaper up my nose it seemed I wasn't in control but the bike carried me, filtering in the dark through the trucks until an hour later it took me beyond the outskirts of the city and into the safety of blackness where there was a quiet spot between two trucks at a truck stop. The blood-letting had stopped and a policeman on duty said I could lie by my bike for a few minutes but not all night because he said it wasn't safe, so I curled up on the ground and slept.

You have to know how India works and how Indians think in order to be safe and I knew it would be a slur on his pride should anything happen to me. The sleep was deep and what felt like hours was only tens of minutes when he woke me and told me to go. Nearby was the sound of men fighting and the policeman began blowing his whistle. Rising sleepily my lips were stuck together with blood that had coagulated and as I wiped my face clean in my mirror, the sound of people running was followed by thwacks of a lathi (stick) on someone's back. Truck drivers are volatile and this is reflected in their driving, and it's impossible for them to wind down, poor sods. Their bosses push them until they are dead with lack of sleep and when the policeman came back he gently pushed me and said to go now so I got on my bike and drove away.

The powders were taking effect and I started to feel less ill. Until this point I'd ridden through the night leaving Mumbai at eight in the evening; I'd driven past Pune and then on through the day to Hyderabad. Temperatures had been in the forties all day and the plan to rush through the city and be well on the way to Vijayawada or maybe Visakhapatnam had failed. Instead there was only the prospect of a second night without sleep as I headed down from higher ground to the river plains around the River Krishma.

Vijayawada on 4th June 2005

I am in Vijayawada. I am following a fast bus. The bus is going really well. This is the sort of ride where you're either writing a foreword or your obituary. But I am flying.

I've recovered completely from really bad dehydration and sunstroke after three hours of rest. I am okay now, and am riding quickly to catch up on time. I think I am on something like a 600 mile schedule. However hard you work in India you're going to lose time, but this is the place where around the world projects gain real credibility, in my view. I am going to ride through the night and try to get to Calcutta by midnight on Sunday.

★ ★ ★ ★ ★

Somewhere here in this beautiful Indian state of Andheri Pradesh I sat on my bike beside a very quiet road. I laid my head down on my tank bag and took my customary nap when I heard a sound I would never forget. There is a tradition in Hindi songs where boy meets girl, they flirt, dance, sing, hold hands and look deeply into each other's eyes, run away and rejoin full of love and devotion, ready to spend the rest of their lives together. The song played from someone's house, several fields away, and was so light and sweet that it sat on the wind like sugar. So sublime was this sound for me that I fell in love with the moment and didn't want to leave. It made me feel so incredibly happy and yet also so terribly sad that I wanted to live forever and I wanted to die there and then. Such a love song makes you smile at tiny thoughts and spread tears across your face at all the lost chances and missed moments. In my dreams, this sound was tugging at me, pulling me, and I knew that if I didn't wake soon it would take me down a dusty track where I would build up speed between the sand and the scrub and ride over a cliff.

As I sat dreaming about riding over a cliff the comparison between this and my last record journey pricked my thoughts. For me, looking around amidst the sound of this music reminded me of what India was like then;

Fastest Man Extract (India) 1997

'...the countryside whisked by in a blur of speed. If there were to be any surprises here they wouldn't be topographical. I had seen it before. Stumpy drought-resistant shrubs lined the road, ochre-coloured soil dipped into valleys browned on the edge of the Western Ghats. High on the Deccan Plateau, copper-coloured citadels of scrawny mountains gritted vertiginous teeth into a sky which presented little complexion, except as a backdrop for the thorny savannah; deep bottle-green set against sepia. It was like riding in one of the film society's old movies; 16mm reality crisping in the sun. Suddenly I felt I was dreaming. Or maybe not dreaming, but overwhelmed by a feeling of being other-worldly; so out of context that it was like being on a different planet...In front of me as I rode was a valley full of flowering trees. Purple-blue jacarandas nestled against clusters of the red and yellow flowers of tamarind, handsome with its short straight trunk and large spreading crown. I liked the trees that lined the roadside because they were now my only view of India and I peered through the scarlet flowers of tulip and coral trees, the light green gul mohurs feathered out like peacocks, as I wound around the empty hilly lanes that ultimately would drop towards the plains far away.

★ ★ ★ ★ ★

20:43 hrs GMT on 4th June 2005

There is a routing problem and I am now heading north up to Calcutta on the Chennai-Calcutta road. This is a section that has not been developed. And it is absolutely terrible. It's the worst road I have ever been on in India in all my driving. My average riding speed here is 17-23 mph. At the moment if I carry on through the night again, which will be the third night in a row, then I'll get into Calcutta at 8 o' clock. If so, I will have lost 12 hours on the record schedule. I have 12 hours, any later and I could lose the whole day. If I lose the whole day, I might have to retire. I am going to ride through the night … and just keep going … and see what I can do.

Near Calcutta on 5th June 2005

I am 350 miles south of Calcutta, the road is very bad – a poor surface that just rocks the bike – it's just not set up for this kind of terrain – smooth road is the bike's natural habitat. Sub sections of expressway were so hot – everything dark - very bad traffic – desperately tired – swollen hands, aching, pains in arms and neck, swollen legs, rash around loins. I need to get to Calcutta by midnight and this will give me a total distance of 1350 to 1400 miles in 2 days and 4 hours or so. It's 4:30 pm local time now. Which, to be honest, will be very good. This will give me 700 miles, apart from the 4 hours. I am very pleased. That means I'll only be 800 miles down on my thousand-miles-a- day schedule. I am on the Chennai-Calcutta highway which is a newly made four lane dual-carriageway. I didn't expect it to be here. Thank God it is! It's a miracle of engineering. It's brilliant, because it's certainly bringing me back to my time. I've just ridden night and day and night and now another day with only a power nap. And now I am going into another night. This will be the end of this stage. So far, so good.

How quickly the memories fade. The downside of the speed of this journey prevents the deep embedding of anything other than primal actions. A crash would never be forgotten, yet another temple or minor conversational impression has to be recorded soon after it takes place or it disappears. Perhaps there is a natural self-selection of events, the least memorable being data filed in some temporary storage space waiting for deletion. I arrived on the outskirts of Calcutta at nine in the morning immediately needing to shit so badly I did it behind a bush beside a busy road and wiped myself clean with grass. Ten minutes later I crossed the new bridge over the Howrah and went straight to the hotel where I always stay, the Fairlawn on Sudder Street by the Indian Museum. The people at the air freighters, Noble Logistics, wouldn't be in the office until around ten so I booked into my room and jumped straight into the bath. The last time I had washed was in

Mumbai. As I scrubbed the dirt off my body I reflected on the statistics of this last ride, which were now normal for this journey: 1450 miles ridden in 2 days 13 hours. Three thirty minute cat-naps, no washing. One small meal, three hours filming, £83 of fuel used at 42 rupees a litre, 10 litres of water drunk, plus 15 packets of electrolytes. India's dirt had turned my bath water black. After 30 minutes' rest I called the freighters and in an extraordinary and unusual feat of forward planning, the crate was already prepared. It just needed my call to have it transported to my hotel, after which the bike would be securely placed inside and the whole package would be trucked within hours of my arrival here to the Cargo Complex at Dum Dum International Airport. When I last shipped a bike it was the size of a large and scruffy dog kennel run by the most relaxed government officials in the world. For 'relaxed', read inept. For inept, read self-serving and corrupt – but not seen.

There would be a period of time when every part of my paperwork would be examined for faults so the possibility of baksheesh could be discussed. The clock, thank goodness, had now stopped, and I could breathe easier. The paperwork was spot on so nothing could impede a quick transit out of India.....But as soon as you say that you are asking the gods to strike you down. Due to the impossibility of removing all of the fuel from the tank, a used motorcycle is classed as a Dangerous Goods Vehicle. The earlier conjecture about Indian customs disallowing such freight had not been an issue so far and neither had the need to separate the tank from the frame. My ticket had been kindly organised by friends of Jiten who had it sent to the hotel with their driver. An Encashment Certificate was needed and also issued and I was given permission to have the freight fly the next night with Thai Airlines on the same flight as me. That evening Kishore, who was in charge of export operations, called and said that the consignment had not been accepted and would be refused onto the flight. He gave me no further details, saying we could discuss it in the morning.

Problems like this occur all the time and after so many journeys I had become fairly sanguine about them. Just then, Namrata, one of Jiten's contacts here in Bengal called me and suggested we hang out, maybe go for a quick boat ride on the river and then have dinner. An excellent way to chill and we ended up off Park Street, the 'Oxford Street' of Calcutta, at a small intimate restaurant the name of which I immediately forgot. Namrata dropped me off at a new guest house which her family had arranged for me to stay at. I really wanted to remain at the Fairlawn but it would have been bad form not to accept their kindnesses. I slept fitfully but felt refreshed when I awoke.

The next morning I took a cab to the freighters', Noble Logistics, an agent acting on behalf of my main agent Expeditors in London. I wanted to know about the problem and Kishore said he would tell me on the way to the airport and ordered his driver to take us to Dum Dum. "You see," he said, "they will not accept the bike because of the battery, it must be taken out." This was not correct and we knew it but Dangerous Goods regulations still had to be followed to the letter. It was absurd that a sealed battery, which had no chance of a spillage, was more critical than a petrol tank which no one had officially checked for content. Maybe, by going along to discuss the situation with the airline, we could avert this crisis. Once we arrived, a slight man with bad teeth, poorly fitting trousers and footwear without any socks was the official in charge of overseeing permits to get into the complex. Until the permit-issuing people arrived to give us temporary passes, we couldn't get in. People here start work around eleven and leave early and when we eventually received the necessary document we went to the office handling the bike. I was ushered in to see the boss of Thai Cargo and we sat quietly for a moment. I asked him if he would allow me to explain the situation. The best way to deal with an Indian person is to show great respect and definitely not make any demands. The 'I insist this should happen' attitude creates a shutdown response and that is absolutely the end of the discussion. The bike would be here for a week. He listened to what I had to say and slowly we made progress. A lower ranking official presented us with a book of regulations for Dangerous Goods and spelled out the different classifications for carrying batteries. I noticed there was a clause which stated that dry batteries are not restricted. "Being a modern battery it contains no sodium and is dry," I said, and everyone looked up. "Of course it's dry, it's not an Enfield you know," I said rather snootily, "it's a Yamaha YZF R1 super sports bike and the technology is very modern". Everyone looked quizzical but seemed willing to accept my explanation. Part of the Indian way is to help as much as possible and I had given everyone a route to show me hospitality without losing face. The paperwork was duly signed off and Kishore called the warehouse where the bike was being stored and told them to bring the bike over immediately as we could now start the next phase: to placate the scrutineers.

Kishore and I went down to the canteen and chatted. After a small meal of chicken and roti, the truck arrived with the bike so we walked across the small yard to customs to finalise the process. Whereas in Perth or Singapore all customs procedures might take as little as an hour, we had been dealing with this issue for nearly two days now. Waiting outside on old chairs, separated from temperatures approaching 45 degrees centigrade by two large industrial fans, we sat quietly.

Having ridden in Dante's Inferno in the midday sun, I noticed I was hardly sweating whilst everyone around was suffering. The boys around me kept saying how hot it was. Cool as a cucumber, I kind of beat them at their own game. This white boy had endured the worst of India's heat and won. On the wall the Terminal Storage and Processing Charges were prominently displayed and underneath the charges, in the Notes to section d), I read the following statement; *Consignments of human remains, coffin including unaccompanied baggage of deceased and Human Eyes will be exempted from the purview of TSP & Demurrage Charges.* So, no charges if you go home in a box; eye balls gratis. Glad we cleared that up then!

I was called over yet again to show customs the engine and the chassis number and this called for the box to be broken open. Once the correct identity of the bike had been established to everyone's satisfaction, the examination could still not be completed until the men from International Security had witnessed it, and they were on a long lunch. If, like everyone else, they started work at ten or eleven, knocked off between twelve until three and then screamed into the complex with great urgency to do a bit of work before pissing off home at four, we might be lucky. But every time we spoke to customs they responded that the necessary final check would be 'in ten minutes'; at such time, the process to clear the bike would be accomplished, but still we waited. Eventually I stood up to a poor little man and told him the Assistant Commissioner would get a piece of my mind if I could ever find his blasted office. Of course, if I did do that, that would completely blow it. Kishore started to shrink into a corner and I began to smell a problem. If I waited just the right amount of time, all would be well, but equally, to wait too long would give out a signal that tomorrow would also be fine. But that would mean the bike would not get on that night's flight and would be stranded for another three days.

Just as I was thinking up a strategy, a man wearing dark glasses arrived. He was 'Security' and demanded that the box be dismantled even though we had established a way to see the engine and chassis numbers perfectly well in between the wooden bars of the case. Had he bothered to inspect the disconnected battery, the deflated tyres or even the small matter of an empty fuel tank, (to which I had no key), I would have understood, but he simply took the numbers and then told the case dismantler to reassemble it. It was so pointless and I said this to the little case dismantler, who had thick horn-rimmed spectacles, yellow teeth but a super sense of humour. "No it's not," he chuckled, in good English, "there are not enough jobs in Calcutta and he has just given me mine!"

Kishore drove me back to my guest house so I could wash my clothes prior to an evening engagement planned with the Chattaraj's. Mr Chattaraj was Senior President of the giant Indian company Adita Birla Group, a cement and mining conglomerate. He travelled to Egypt every month and handled the company's expansive business strategy with countries as diverse as Thailand, Australia and the US. Before that he was with British Oxygen and basically climbed up the corporate ladder with enormous success. Yet he was extremely modest. Eva, his wife, was a full time mum, and their daughter Namrata had been my companion occasionally over the past 24 hours. We talked over a meal of chicken keema and yoghurt and enjoyed some delicious mango slices and gula sweets. I said something about Mr Gandhi in relation to this project and it was politely ignored. I was obviously not making any sense but, as I pointed out, at least I was *trying* not to make sense of a situation which had no sense, instead of just not making sense – there was a difference! Afterwards they hailed a cab and I was driven to the airport to fly to Bangkok.

FIRST CONVERSATION IN THAILAND

I flew into Bangkok overnight from Calcutta and touched down early in the morning. Somehow I had managed to secure four empty seats and after a pretty stiff curry lay down to sleep. Due to a frighteningly big Indian chap behind me who snored all the way until we landed, I ended up a mess. I only had hand luggage so escaped quickly and caught a cab into town. I'd planned to have breakfast with a friend who didn't turn up so I booked into my usual hotel on Khaosan Road and went to my room and slept for an hour. By eleven I was back-tracking to the Cargo Complex at Bangkok's airport. Nipon, the freighting agent in the city office told me whom to meet and when I arrived I was introduced to Mr Larpawat, a nice, smiling comfortable-looking man who immediately made me feel at ease, and we got straight down to business.

"I have a carnet, so it should be easy" I said, opening positively as if to ward off evil customs spirits.

"Yes," he said

"And my passport," I said.

"Yes."

"Well, I have one,"

"Yes."

"So that should be all you need?" I continued, trying to elicit something from the inscrutable one.

"Yes."

"So Mr Laraprat, we don't anticipate any problems?" beginning to wonder if he or I was actually in the wrong building. Maybe he didn't work here, or was the cleaner and was just being polite. "You are Mr Laraprat aren't you?"

"Larpawat."

"Don't you mean 'no?'I said, meaning 'no' to problems, 'yes' to who he was!

"Er yes,"

"What!." I was getting into it now. "Is that all you say?"

"Yes, er no,"

"About the problems or who you are?"

"Yes, no,"

"What?"

"No problems."

"Great," so throwing caution to the wind, I said, "When can I have my bike?"

"I am Larpawat, pleased to meet you," and held out his hand.

"We've done that and the pleasure's all mine," knowing he'd not crack the irony.

"Tea?"

"No." The tea arrived.

"That more of problem."

Here we go. "Oh?" I said.

"Yes, I have never seen carnet before, please explain."

★ ★ ★ ★ ★

The roundabout of international relations where countries make war or embrace is based on two people not understanding each other, speaking as if they were in-between mouthfuls of rice. If they rolled up their trousers and instead stood in the paddy field where the rice grew under a sweltering sun, they would soon get the idea that discussions should be brief and to the point. Instead of being down-hearted, I had taught myself always to look at the options: either (1) an around the world motorcyclist journeying at speed and getting paid to do it is very lucky – wonderful sights and peoples – the joy of said international relations and spiritual harmony; or (2) one rides like a dervish

I'm about to leave and am being filmed in my home village in Wales. My eldest son Willow Indian Summer looks like he's a record breaker in waiting!

Tatyana Gazelle age 4, and Juno Jupitor age 6. Hen and me had 3 children between trips, and then I had to go away again!

Nick On...

FAME

'Fame must be like this. When I stop I am surrounded by about a hundred people who almost cut off my air. They make it hard to breathe. In the last town, there were so many people waiting for me to come out I began to realise what it must be like to be famous and I wasn't sure I liked it. It killed what wind there was and made me feel like a small sailing boat in an ocean of people who made my air too hot to breathe.'

One of the world's two most populated countries and the crush continues.

The heat in Hyderabad nearly overwhelmed me.

Nick On...

HEAT

'In India I was on the point of passing out, I had to keep finding places with air-conditioning to cool down in. My body was overheating. I was beyond the point where I could drink water to cool down. My face was bright red. There were various things about this journey where an ordinary motorcyclist might have had a heart attack.'

Nick On...

HYGIENE
'The longest period for which I didn't take my clothes off was six days. I'm not a sweaty person. After a while you don't get any dirtier. And I'm in an environment where it doesn't matter, so I don't care.'

OX CARTS

A motorcycle takes you to faraway places where time is sometimes faster or slower. There are places in the world where ox carts have not yet been replaced by combustion engines, and there are other places where people never feel the heat of the sun on their back because there is a corridor of air-conditioning that connects them from their bed to their office and back.

I once rode around the world on an Indian Enfield... let's put it this way, it was a different type of journey to that of riding an R1!

Given that there are no rules of the road, Indian drivers are actually quite good, it's just that nuts fall off steering columns and trucks end up taking a detour.

Nick On...

LOW POINTS

'The low points happen sporadically every day, depending on your emotional state. Doubts about the trip are the low points. Is it credible? Is it worthy? Is it necessary? Does anyone care? These are the questions about life itself. The mechanics of it are easy compared with that.'

Tim and the lads at Wright's Bike Shop in Salt lake City. They did a great service and I was back on the road within 30 minutes.

Nick On...

SCENERY

'You don't get time to look at the scenery, but it's like speed reading – you absorb it and you can reflect on it later.'

Somewhere in Peru, 1996. Riding from Tierra del Fuego to Alaska in 30 days gave me the riding lesson of my life.

Parts of Australia were like a Norman Rockwell painting, all nostalgic and 1950's, a kind of place where time stood still.

Like Whales being the biggest mammals, at 153 metres, Australian Road Trains must be amongst the biggest form of transport on the road.

Signpost Forest at Watson Lake along the Alaskan Highway.

Nick On...

NOT TAKING A MAP
'It was a mistake. In the States I don't need maps, but in India road signs are in Hindi or Urdu so you ask three Indians for directions and go with the majority. I got lost in New Zealand and went the wrong way for 150 miles. I felt stupid. But I'm not a military-planning sort of person.'

EATING AND DRINKING

'I tend not to eat or drink very much when I'm riding. I lost a stone in weight on this journey. If you drink too much coffee you just piss down the road. Your body tells you what you need. Eat too much and you want to sleep, eat too little and you start to fade away.'

Kangaroo kill was my worst fear. From the point of view of animals, Australia is the most dangerous country in the world to ride across at night.

Nick On...

TIREDNESS AND CONCENTRATION

'The worst thing you can do is have nothing going on in your head. So I have a discussion going on in my head – I ask myself why do I do this journey. Does this have any meaning?

'You're a prisoner in your helmet. I can't stop riding, I can't afford to stop concentrating. So my mind becomes my freedom – your body and mind will always find ways of expanding.'

'You get to the point where you think you can do anything – it might be endomorphins, a physiological high. It only comes after several hundred miles. Towards the end I float.'

Psychologists might say that it's dangerous, that I'm fooling myself – but how can they possibly know what it's like? They haven't done it.'

On the Stuart Highway. I'd just missed Dinky's performance. I made a note to go back the following year!

With a fuel capacity of 17 litres and a total mileage capability of between 145 and 200 miles depending on my speed, there were still areas at night when gas stations had closed or didn't exist at all.

Nick On...

SPEED

'Coming into Calais on the last stretch I did 160mph, but for most of the journey I didn't go very fast because I didn't want to stress the bike. There was always traffic, apart from in Australia where in the Northern Territories there is no speed limit and I rode as fast as a could. The only time I went under the speed limit was when I was asleep.'

Mike Maines at Don's Motorcycle Shop in Anchorage. A superb tyre and chain change. I used two chains and four sets of tyres during the whole journey.

"Shortly after meeting Hennie in 1996 I rode the length of the Americas on a red Triumph Daytona 900cc. I started by riding from Buenos Aires to Ushuaia in Tierra del Fuego on the southernmost tip of the continent, but I fell off in snow before I even got there. I knew it was coming because the front wheel had slid three times and I'd only just managed to hold it. What on earth possessed me to think that I had the experience to ride in those conditions, on standard road tyres? Lying on the road, cushioned by the snow, looking up at the moon, in pain, I lay there blinking and sort of smiled, wondering how I was going to explain to the sponsors that it was all over before I'd even got to the start line. All I wanted was a free sports bike and it was preposterous the lengths I was prepared to go to, to get one."

Loneliness of the Long Distance Biker

all day and night missing things that squash whilst trying to make sense of a blurred landscape with occasional snatched glances of incredible things. All of this is punctuated with lots of time hanging around buildings poorly constructed of pre-cast concrete, trying to be nice to some customs official, while knowing that all he wants to do is find fault and an excuse to extract some money out of you to support his menial salary.

After another chat with Laraprat I was completely confused and caught a cab back to the hotel feeling another long wait coming on. Opposite the reception to the Buddy Lodge where I was staying there was an excellent Internet café run by a very confused young man. He was definitely a young man but walked and talked like a girl. But his Internet connections were fast and he didn't diddle my change. So I uploaded more diary and book excerpts for Jiten to put up on the website. A few emails came in and I managed to send short replies. Messages were coming through that Elderflowers were starting to blossom around my house in Wales, and while normally that would tug at my homesick heart, just now it represented a dangerous loss of focus. Distilling abstract feelings of home into a purer describable form allows you to neutralise sentiment, a skill worth learning. It is the ability to withstand the thumping dull ache of being hospitalised emotionally that allows you to travel well.

My old motor biking pal, Daniel Vetter, eventually rearranged his schedule to meet me that evening but meanwhile I had been asked by Laraprat to call at four in the afternoon. I braced myself for bad news. Customs would say they couldn't look at the bike today, and that would mean tomorrow which, being Friday, meant the whole thing risked slipping into the weekend. Why bother? This was becoming too much of a drag. The physical issue of riding was in danger of being submerged by the technical processes of dragging this damn machine through the world's customs areas. It was turning into a Herculean and Kafka-esque task with very bad karma. I had forgotten how frustrating it could be to get a motorcycle through all these borders and I suddenly felt the journey wasn't as cool as I wanted it to be. With more time, it's fine to hang about, but it was getting harder to restart than to keep going. Every decision, every bit of energy, every single tiny action to keep this show on the road, was down to me; out here in pre-monsoon temperatures with 80% humidity and Dante's Inferno traffic from hell. Shit, shit and *shit* once again.

Given the angst-making nature of such a journey it made me think how much I have been programmed by my ancestors to survive. I am constantly in a state of worry about time and schedules, whether the bike will stand up to the strain or whether I will have to endure some life-threatening collision. In the same way that homeopathic treatments can be diluted to the point where only a residual memory of a long-gone potion remains in the water, I have somehow gained some evolutionary advantage from my forebears which has given me the ability to disregard the here and now and focus on the future. Those who worry less about what will happen next are gored by the unforeseen. If you don't plan for the rabid dog entering your den, how are you going to know how to fend it off?

Diary The Next Day – Friday 10th June
Sitting in the taxi I feel nervous. This is odd because this next stage from Bangkok to Singapore is nearly perfect for the R1. The route is largely good and the Malay stretch is excellent. Yet my stomach is turning over. I can feel the pressure building because soon we will know exactly how we stand in relation to the 1000 miles per day record. I can just do what I can. Can't understand how well I have

been feeling. The stop-start nature of the journey is really hard to deal with – it's the only way to do this project. As soon as the bike needs to fly it's out of my control. Difficult to keep up a steady rhythm – guess that is the hard part which not everyone can handle. I'm afraid this inconsistency will sap my huge reserves energy and then I will collapse. I am not confident about anything. 1200 miles or more in one session is a lot. Yet because the bench mark has been raised it has to feel possible. It allows for no stops and no sleep apart from power naps.

When I got to the cargo terminal I couldn't find the agent's office then luckily I found a business card containing the address. I was really trying to do too much at once; get the bike released, find out where to go, call back to the office, call ahead to confirm my next flight, get the crates made, tanalise the wood and then secure an appointment for the bike to be brought into the next customs process. I could not lose anything, nor could I get homesick, also money had to be monitored, the business had to be maintained back home and the kids needed long phone calls from their Dad. I did not have anyone out here to help. I made all the calls. I did all the business. I did all the riding.

Like anyone who juggles their lives, their business with their family, I sometimes have to sit in quiet corners and take deep breaths. Like everyone else, I sometimes wake and feel I cannot function anymore and that the world is going to cave in. And like most people I occasionally close my eyes and hope that when I open them again my life will be easier. That's what happened on this day in Thailand. Mr Laraprat told me the bike had been released by customs and would be available immediately after lunch. Clearly he wasn't the cleaner after all and had operated more efficiently than any of my other air freighters. He'd just got on with the job with no fuss. I wanted to hug him, but thought that might be misconstrued, so I just said "Thanks very much!" The upside to this quick delivery would be that 24 hours from the start in Bangkok I should arrive in Singapore. The horrendous motorbike jam from Johor across the Causeway would not be my problem. At the normal rush hour periods, tens of thousands of bikes and mopeds squeeze across the bridge that links Malaysia to Singapore in conditions so miserable you wouldn't inflict them on a caged bird.

I thought I'd be winging my way across Bangkok city, the stink of the traffic in my face, in no time. Then Mr Laraprat asked me if I wanted lunch and I said no. Five minutes later a small tray of food arrived. Outside, rain clouds gathered. There was no chance of evading poor weather as the rainy season had just begun. Having ridden up and down the Malay Peninsula eight times I have never stayed dry or properly seen the mountainous region around Ipoh – only sheet lightning ever seems to illuminate what is one of the most breathtaking sections of motorway in the world.

Bangkok

Thought I was going to get held up again in Bangkok but amazingly Expeditors got me through in a day. I arrived on the Thursday morning at 06.20 after a late 02.10 overnight flight from Calcutta and the bike was waiting for me at noon on Saturday. This is possibly the fastest customs activity I have ever had and transitions like this increase the credibility of the trip. I want to get home as fast as possible. There will be many opportunities for me to hang around such beautiful spots in the world but only one last chance to become the fastest solo motorcyclist around the world. Now I can concentrate on riding a sports bike on excellent roads. The 700 or so miles across Thailand are good and the 700 odd miles across Malaysia are excellent and will allow me a high average. I'll be very disappointed if I don't complete this in 24 hours and so recover around 400 miles. That will make me only 600 miles behind the 1000 miles per day schedule.

After lunch, Laraprat took me to the bike and I broke down the crate, loaded up and rode off to the nearest garage where I put air into my partly deflated tyres. Laraprat followed me and gave me a bottle of water. For a moment I thought he was going to be overly sentimental.

"It's OK Laraprat, I know what I'm doing, please don't worry."

"Not worried," and he still stood there.

"Don't get all sentimental then!" I said laughing.

"Not that."

"Well, what then?" There was a long pause with something of impending relief about him.

"My name Larpawat," and he smiled.

"Yes, Laraprat."

"No, *wat* not prat," and he gave me a bottle of water and left.

Something else we cleared up then.

★ ★ ★ ★ ★

It took an hour to get out of Bangkok. The traffic was moving and I got pulled over by the cops for being in the wrong lane. The policeman stooped and laughed at me and then whispered, *'100 bahts,'* which is about £1.50 and I was thinking about giving it to him when his attention was distracted by another cop on a bike who had just waved to me, and was probably his boss. Not only was I without GPS but without a map. I'd forgotten that gas stations in these parts don't stock such things and with only one major road running on a north – south axis I had simply memorised the route: Ratchaburi, Hua Hin, Prachuap Khiri Khan, Chumphon and Sadou.

On the road in Thailand

Riding as hard as possible before dark I managed to cover 200 miles. It was a pretty paltry amount and I didn't feel I'd done enough to stay on schedule but carried on. It's odd how the early miles seem to take longer than those at the end of the ride. Once night fell everything slowed down. My night vision was never great and had deteriorated over the years. Throttle and braking response was still quick, balance and general flexibility was good, spatial awareness in traffic excellent; I was cautiously fast, although paranoid in the corners but more than all of this, my ability to endure had improved more than I had dared to imagine. My biggest fear about attempting such a journey nine years on was that I might fail with a complete loss of credibility. I honestly didn't know if I could do it. Self-belief is only half the story. There is a point when you are too old to be young but too young to be old. It's a pivotal position when you either write the foreword or the obituary to the next part of your life and just then I didn't know which was my destiny.

Apart from having enough skill to stay upright, the most important attribute needed to successfully complete a project like this is endurance, which is simply a question of dislocating from the pain. If part of that pain is physical, we are told to visualise the opposite, so in my mind I imagined what it was like to float. When you hear of winners heading towards the line, they tell you it no longer hurts. They say you fly like the wind and everything is clear. At such rare times, it's almost *other worldly* and it becomes impossible to fail. There are times when any biker feels like this. When in your helmet you are smiling so much your cheeks cramp. In your helmet you are laughing with the joy of riding and although it sounds unbelievable, every real motorcyclist knows it to be true; that in between all the hard times, when it doesn't work out, when all around you is grey, there are those few occasions when absolutely nothing is better than riding your bike and you ride on automatic, while thoughts about your life fly past in your head.

For me, as I sped south down the Malay Peninsula, I thought of my youth – it had flown past; these twenty five years on the road had been long and hard. As the essence of my life had been passed on to me so it would with my own sons and daughter. In a way I felt sorry for the joy they would feel because nothing, yet nothing worth having comes without pain.

As I changed up from an anonymous set of lights, accelerated to second, held the clutch in and lazily slipped through the gears to top, I settled down to a rhythm. The bike sounded sweet with nothing out of place, every nut and bolt still tight and delirious fun to ride. Sometimes, in tiny moments of hysteria, you just shout out into the night, standing on the pegs. For a second you want every biker you know to be with you because just then you feel so high but so alone. On a journey like this you are so free, but there is no one there to share what you see and smell.

The night wore on. The sweet sickly scent of durian trees came and went whilst the strawberry liqueur of rambutan drifts around fruit stalls which sit like homely beacons to travellers on the side of this long dark road. Thoughts steadied to a more sedate level. The road was so black it could have been the sky, until we bypassed a town – a few orange lights, dogs scattering - so you stay awake and you think of anything that comes to mind. What was it about that first French flat, that first love, the first smell of girl, the first blond in the blue sports car, the laughing, the happiness, so many firsts of everything, that hay barn, the straw in your hair; that hot summer when everything simmered then burnt, when the earth cracked and the hand pumps croaked; emotional salts so strong it sears the brain.

As I rode hard into the dark my thoughts were not of now and I cared even less for what lay ahead. The future commissioned hard times; making money, paying the bills, feeding the babies. So much were the thrills of my journeys interlocked with the precariousness of earning a living that travelling sometimes gave me no solace, but when it did, there was nothing under the sun that inspired me more. I thought of home, my children and whether they remembered me and how, then instantly clicked back into the ride. Overhead signs put you back to where you need to be. Youths waved me into position as I slowed to gas up my high octane animal in a country filling station. The bike sits there quietly. She is like a racehorse sipping her fuel, just waiting. Without the cushion of wind to separate my legs from her hot engine we both feel the heat; reminded how hard it was, both of us working at our maximum. We knew it wasn't all to do with speed. It was agility and balance; traction, strength, power, torque and style. It all happened in darkness so black you couldn't see your hand in front of your face, yet at every turn, every bump, we knew where we were, my bike and I. She kept me alive. How grateful can you be for that? Her superb machinery kept me safe. If just for a moment the bike could be considered the principal character in this story, it was a brief part because she quickly transcended that, and became instead my key to whatever glory was ever meant to be mine.

And so we floated across Thailand, my R1 almost driving by itself, it let me fill my head with thoughts about this and that; that first house when every corner was a pleasure to fill; the girlfriends who said they loved me and left; the wives who said they'd stay with you forever then didn't; the babies that slipped into your arms, all bloody with their cords that you bit free with your teeth. All these thoughts made me smile in my helmet. And then there were the moments when your heart broke, so many times when you went away and came back to both joy and sadness. Such things are part of journeying and cram all travellers' heads as they did mine as we raced through the night, the R1 and me; past small lights and market stalls piled high with exotic fruits from tiny lithe women with their generous smiles, these mothers, all of them, unsure whether I am lover or son. So you stop, greet, buy, leave and ride on as fast as you dare in the darkness. The night stays for hours and there is no stopping other than to re-fuel. No eating, just drinking. Hardly looking, just thinking. This is how it was for me riding across Thailand at speed at night, waiting for rain that never came, not even before the dawn when a blue greyness quickly wiped away the black and I arrived all sweaty and steaming at the border where I bade good morning to officials who remembered me from the last time I passed this way. The motorway along Malaysia was smooth and fast.

In the *fastest man* journey, I heard different things than this journey. Then I stopped to listen and look around, now I stopped only to fuel up my bike and start riding again.

Fastest Man Extract (Malaysia 1997)

Towering flashes of lightning lit and shadowed gigantic plugs of tree-covered rock, making them stand out like sentinels for the gods of the jungle that embraced the winding highway. In between the geological rifts, deep in the jungle, in the old days of gin and Jaguar settlers, the tea-planters and vegetable farmers would have hauled their way up these mountain roads. Hawk eagles and brahminy kites soared from rift to rift. Crested firebacks and racquet-tailed drongoes with sweeping tails stood next to saffron-coloured orioles. Wagtails flitted and mynahs stood with the hoarsely-coughing flower-peckers. Weaver birds hung from their tubular nests. During the day monitor lizards basked on the hard shoulder and at night frogs belched for king and country. In the jungle there is never silence but neither is there in the desert, where scarab beetles can be heard scratching over the sand.

* * * * *

Diary Entry: Bangkok to Singapore
Start time: 14.30 Friday 9th June
Finish time: 14.00 Saturday 10th June
Distance: 1250 miles

I don't know if it's getting easier or harder. Must be to do with perception because I imagined this stage would be easy but it wasn't. Must stop comparing with India because that was the ultimate test of riding, but the 1250 miles down to here had me wondering if I really was up to this journey. I wanted more mileage and a faster time by an hour or so but filming soaks up at least an hour a day if not more. The only reason I can film is because I don't sleep. Still, the up side is that if I am using the 1000 miles per day as my standard, then it looks as if I've shaved 200 miles off my 1000 mils debit, so I am only 800 miles down. If I don't panic, I won't push my luck and ride badly or hit an animal. If I take it carefully, but quick, I can take a bit off here and there and try to start the USA on level pegging.

If sense prevails in Singapore then it would surprise me. Although this little city state is one of my favourite countries, the more you try to do things the more you realise it's a city run on compliance. The ride across the Causeway was simple enough and the entry through Primary Clearance alongside the moped boys in the motorbike channel didn't take long, but in addition to getting my carnet stamped I also needed a plastic card from the Land Transport Authority. A daily levy is paid by all vehicles driving within Singapore and also by any vehicles that enter from outside. A chip-encoded card has to be obtained and loaded with cash to coincide with the estimated number of days you think you might be staying. If the levy is not paid, it continues to accrue even though you might have exported the vehicle, so one day the offender will get a bill for several thousand dollars without even having had the pleasure of being here. So I sat in a windowless air-conditioned office waiting for various officers to deal with my case. Once upon a time entry here took minutes, now it had the potential for taking half a day. I couldn't chase around any more, I was so tired. Fortunately, I was processed very efficiently, after which I would drop off my bike in the holding bay prior to customs examination. If there was a cooling off period, and there usually was, the bike would not be able to leave until Monday, so by the time I returned from sorting out the paperwork here at the border and then later at the airport, I could not expect to be in my room before six in the evening. If only travelling life was that easy. The Chief Vehicle Import Executive, Mr Wan, suddenly turned up, clutching my carnet and said that because I had arrived on a Saturday I could not enter Singapore, and the conversation went like this:

"It's Saturday and you cannot ride in Singapore," said Mr Wan.

"Why?"

"Because the AA is closed, you cannot buy an International Circuit Permit and therefore you can't get insurance."

"So why can't I buy insurance here at the border?"

"You can't, because there is no facility."

"But you are being very strict about everything else and yet not providing appropriate services for travellers such as myself?"

"Yes, that is true."

"In every country in the world I have travelled to there is a facility to allow a vehicle in, and most often with insurance."

"Yes, so?"

"So, if Singapore is the big and clever place it's supposed to be why doesn't it sell such things? After all, you've only got two land borders, it's hardly difficult."

Silence. I'd put the poor chap on the spot and he was only really trying to help. He had the authority to send me back to

Johor and re-enter on Monday and start the whole fancy process again, but as I was here and the bike was technically impounded until the paperwork was sorted out, I agreed to a tow truck to transport it directly to the airport where it could stew in the bonded warehouse until customs had well and truly fingered it. The only difference was that I didn't ride the last part across Singapore, but that brief twenty mile mileage won't be recorded anyway. It's probable that this could have been arranged in advance, but it would have meant sending the original carnet and passport weeks in advance to the AA at the risk of these getting lost, and as I only had the bike two weeks before I left I couldn't get the carnet until two days before the start. Also, the previous time I did this it required someone to personally sign the paperwork, so it was a lost cause.

Singapore

Rode 1250 miles from Bangkok to Singapore in exactly 24 hours so I have made up 200 miles - better than nothing - so I reckon I'm approximately 800 miles down on a 1000 mile a day schedule. Plus, as the previous team record is about 19,000 and something miles in 19 days 8 hours I also need to gain 500 miles and half a day. As I am riding really well I am confident, but one mistake and it's all over. There's so much still to do it's scary and it all has to be ridden perfectly. The standards of the game have been raised and I enjoy the opportunity to do likewise. The Thailand section was in the night, 80% good roads, not a motorway and not as fast as I remember but so much better than India. I could only speed up in Malaysia. Australia will give us some 'like for like' roads and I hope to make up another 50 miles a day - 300 miles - plus an overnight to Sydney from Melbourne. There's less chance of hitting a Kangaroo on that section, so I might make up 200 miles, an extra 500 in total, so I should be only 300 miles behind. Then I shall still have to make up an extra 500 miles and lose half a day if I am to beat the present team record, in which case it'll all be down to going for it on the last leg and I want 1200 miles a day on that. I'm actually enjoying it but it is hot, very dangerous in the wrong hands and just one thing going wrong messes it all up - the book, the film and the PR - quite a pressure. It's Sunday now and I have a day off while the bike goes through customs. It should be out tomorrow (Monday) when I hope to fly immediately to Perth to prepare for the arrival of the bike. At least I can film here while I'm waiting. I hope people appreciate my little story; I don't suppose they all will, but what the hell, it's a life that's been lived as best I know how.

HOW TO GET A FREE
GIN SLING AT RAFFLES

When I eventually arrived in town, I quickly found cheap digs at a small but well known chain of budget hotels called Hotel 81. It was located on the Balestier road on the way to Thompson Road, just a little out from the centre. Interestingly it was next door to the Fragrance Hotel which had neon signs saying *'Roses'* and late at night a queue of taxis waited with their flashers on. It would appear that this is a very short time 'love hotel' where you can buy a room by the hour. Sitting in the lobby, there were several 'whities' with really average looks accompanied by stunningly beautiful local girls; those guys must have had the most remarkable wit and intelligence to attract such partners. After a quick meal across the road I plunged into the shower and slept soundly until midday. As it was Sunday and the bike was impounded until Monday I had a day free. (On Monday it was scheduled to be crated up and despatched to Perth). As usual, all my spare time was spent filming or writing. I took the 124 bus to Orchard Road where there was an Internet Café in the Cineplex. From there I could file my diary reports and check my mail. By the time the light had faded I was on the number 14 bus to Raffles Hotel. I entered the hotel from the back, past the Long Bar and started filming. Someone in a white costume and high collar asked me not to use a tripod and suggested I speak to the manager who promptly came down to the lobby to explain that the hotel, being a national monument, could not be filmed without permission. I knew he had a job to do and told him a little story about how, twenty years ago, I had a liaison with a girl who, I was reliably informed, was a niece of Mr Lee Kuan Yew, the man in charge of the country. Singaporeans don't blush, they have the wrong colour, but before I could tell him about the time I had with the Arts Officer from the British Council, the hotel fellow said that as there was a dress code would I mind sitting quietly in the Writers' Bar where he kindly offered me a drink. He clearly didn't know quite what to make of me.

I sat quietly, and in the absence of anyone to talk to, told myself my own anecdotes once again. The last time I stayed here was in 1982, having just bicycled the length of Indonesia. I'd given up university to do this, which is code for admitting that I failed all my second year exams because I was going out with a Singaporean girl who never wore any knickers. The Chairman of the bicycle company had sponsored me but the Managing Director had absconded with his wife and all the company funds, so when I got to Singapore there wasn't any of the promised money waiting for me. My parents hadn't any cash to bail me out so desperate measures were required and I persuaded the then manager of Raffles to let me have a suite in return for some publicity. I called up the Miss Singapore Model Agency to loan me a few girls on the same sketchy basis. A photographer friend I met in Bali arranged to meet me in town and then shot us hanging outside the old Beach Road lobby and the image was sent to as many newspapers in the area that we knew. The manager was so pleased he extended my stay for a week and, worryingly for the nation, introduced me to his daughter, who was the then Prime Minister's niece.

In those days, if you went out with the boss's daughter, everything was on the house. Twenty five years on, I had most graciously been offered a complimentary Gin Sling and now resided in a small, smart budget 'love hotel' just a five dollar cab ride down the road. The irony of this was not lost on me. In a film I had recently seen by Wang Lei Wei called *The Hand* the director tells a story about unrequited love, declining youth and the predictable fall from favour. The film tells of the impossible love affair a beautiful woman had with her tailor, for only a tailor can touch a woman like a lover without actually consummating the relationship. Over the years, she, a beautiful young courtesan, had her tailor make the finest dresses so she could impress her wealthy suitors who would pay her bills and keep her in the lifestyle she chose. In time, her measurements were not what they were and although the tailor hid her measurements from her, the suitors began to stay away. With no one to pay the rent she ends up working on the waterfront, taking sailors for pennies and before long falls consumptive. The tailor was in love with her from the beginning and apart from a final tryst, she was to die in the gutter, their love unrequited.

What strikes me is how, once the first half of your life has elapsed, it plays the ghost to the second half, and is inevitably second best. Lying on my bed in a room barely larger than the bed itself, it wasn't difficult to feel privileged. It wasn't a suite; there wasn't a sofa and desk; no long walk across a large room to a large television, no view of the city at night: no porter, no calls home, no mini-bar, nothing but a bed, a small TV, wash basin and toilet; but neither was there a hedge shielding the old version of a younger me from the wind, or a tarpaulin to protect me from the rain; there was no concrete dust on a building site and no need to look for abandoned buildings where it was possible to lie safely; there were no backs of cars, no motels stinking of stale beer and vomit or whore-houses, bodily fluids and floors of people who pretended to be a friend; and while there are times in life when it seems devoid of glamour, at least it was warm and dry and no one was going to hurt me.

AUSTRALIA

The next morning I took a bus to the subway and the MRT to Changi Airport. A cab took me to the Cargo Complex to start customs formalities once again. I wasn't anticipating any delays and the bike was expected to fly out within 24 hours. The Yamaha dealer in Perth had been notified and a new supply of Road Attack tyres ordered from Continental, ready to be fitted the moment I arrived. To keep up with the record no more time could be lost and a schedule that included Perth to Sydney via Alice Springs had to be accomplished in less than five days. Highway 1 would give the project more miles and was exactly the same route I used in 1997; it still meant a daily average of 1100 miles each day. That was respectably tough but completely possible. The tougher task was to maintain sufficient motivation to want to continue. This wasn't self pity but a real examination into the needs and processes of the human spirit:

"Do you think it a worthless thing to do?" I said to my imaginary Interviewer.

"No, but the rationale behind it needs to be explained. Once you have the explanation of why, you can begin to create the reason."

"There are lives to be saved, real altruistic issues that projects like this don't address at all,"

"You might not be able to in an obvious way, but people are clever, they take the bits they want from the whole. Altruism exists only because it is essential for the human condition to survive and if, in someone's dreamscape, they become inspired, that's not a bad thing."

"Accepted, but what can possibly be seen to be altruistic about a journey like this?"

"Forget altruism, that's not the job of the journey; just accept that this is a hard task – it is not a holiday – accept that such journeys have the opportunities to create an alternative empathy with others.

After all, capitalism, democracy, call it what you like, everything represents a choice of calling."

"Calling?"

"Well, some people don't want to follow the regular route and journeys like this and many others before and after create a different way for people to follow, even if it's only in their quiet thoughts."

"There is a view that if you think it needs explaining, then it really is an unknown or misunderstood concept."

"OK, but everything needs explaining at first, that's why we have teachers. The first mountaineers, the first sailors, even the first motorcyclists, showed us what could be done and others followed. Like entertainers, the balladeers with their love songs, they transport us – it's all to do with being taken to another place; they take us away from certain mundanities in our lives for a short while. Think of it like a punctuation in reality."

"People go to work in jobs they hate and retire maybe four or five years before they die. There are more absurd things than adventures but because people in work fit into a more functionalist paradigm, they are more acceptable than so-called adventurers could ever be."

This mental conversation was frustrating. Entirely make-believe, it was born out of an intellectual deadlock created in part by geographical isolation. With no one to refer to, no one with whom to lock into some dialectic, there is only so much anyone on a journey can dig down into themselves. I called a friend and she sent me an email:

Email Monday June 13th Anon

'Pushing boundaries is a very important and inspiring thing and there are a lot of people who do this and pull even more along in their wake who in turn are inspired in ways that enrich their own lives and they in themselves inspire others, like a snowball effect. Whether it's in art or sport or philosophy, the endeavours that are really on the edge pull the middle to a more exciting place - there has to be something or

someone to react to – someone who strives for what seems impossible. This was so much more the case 100 years ago and now our culture is so wrapped up in safety nets that we forget how to live by intuition. There are whole countries who do not want a nation of adventurous unmanageable people who think for themselves. Only a few people are capable of living on that edge with integrity. I can't imagine theirs is a choice not to do it if you are capable of it and I am sure it's lonely sometimes.'

Perth, Australia
The challenge of going around the world fast on a motorcycle has changed considerably since 1997 and it won't actually be possible to do it for much longer. The cost is becoming prohibitive and post "9/11" the amount of paperwork has seriously increased as has the time it takes to get the bike through customs. Also, this event has become very professional, unlike when I instigated it eight years ago. Then, I just went for the previous record of 33 days by car and beat it by a couple of days - it was more relaxed than now. The bike got held up in quarantine but is now released and I am all set to pick it up tomorrow before 07.00 and I start my first full day in Australia. Very nervous about the wildlife even though I've been here many times before - it never gets easier and the 'roos and emus are of course impossible to predict. Some night riding is needed but hopefully not too much. I have no predictions about my time around Australia but I am going for the fastest safe time I am capable of. Will call in to the office a couple of times a day and try to do some filming but it will be a squeeze. My head is good though and I'm looking forward to completing the fourth stage safely. Met a brilliant bloke called Trevor who is one of Australia's leading bike journalists. He put me up for a couple of days

I left Perth city in the morning. Everything was in order and there was enough fuel to get me to a petrol station. It was dark and it was raining and Trevor led me out of town in his utility vehicle, Someone called Neil rode with me for a while but found it hard going wearing his sunnies and turned back.

Trevor went like a rocket and I followed – it was so helpful and he led for about 100 miles.

Saturday Perth to 268 kms south of Port Hedland

As the darkness drew away so daylight could take its place, a landscape of open farming country slowly presented itself through a veil of thinly spread mist. A few hours north of Perth, after Trevor had left me and returned back to his comfortable home in his Ute, I stopped in a café to drink a cup of tea. The small café was on the way to Meekatharra and was distinguished only by the fact that there was no one who really wanted to talk to me. Everything about it was forgettable There was a fridge near the counter, four square tables with wooden chairs, nothing on the walls other than off-yellow emulsion paint and a door with an irritating bell which rang whenever anyone entered or left. The ordinariness of this café was what set it apart from everything else in my life which at that moment felt extraordinary. I was alone for weeks at a time, hardly spoke a word all day. I was far away from home, unknown, and was riding solo around the world on a motorcycle in a cumulative time faster (I hoped) than anyone had managed before on our busy little planet.

That was not so extraordinary if you compare it to a man like Alexander von Humboldt who spent five years in the Americas travelling 15,000 kilometres while identifying 600 new species of fauna and collecting 1600 plants. What's the connection? It's to do with the relativity of 'extraordinariness'. Just when you think you are extraordinary, you are not. I once cycled the length of South America but having explored the northern coastline and the interior, Humboldt was actually responsible for completely redrawing the map of South America which I was using. He was a really extraordinary man who, being a gifted physicist, geographer and geologist also mapped the stream systems connecting the Rio Negro and the Orinoco, measured the effects of air pressure and altitude on vegetation and studied kinship in the Amazon Basin. Apart from his biographies and volumes of work, he was also the first person to discover that the earth's magneticism declined in intensity the further you were away from the poles and that was his overriding achievement.

As I sat there in that café, looking at the fridge before glancing out of the window, mysteriously thinking about this man Humboldt, I suddenly felt less extraordinary. There was a small modest parallel however. Like him I too planned to spend the next 20 years writing up my life's work and even though it might not extend to 30 volumes, there would be some philosophical thoughts that might make the odd reader scratch his head. This book does not have anything to do with comparing the salinity of water between the Atlantic and the Pacific, nor with discovering sea currents, but it does look at the way one man sat in a café wondering why the lack of soft furnishings made it easier to leave. It would have been unimaginably sad had this café been equipped with sofas, the Sunday newspapers and a charming hostess who might lean over me at close quarters and ask me if there was anything else I would like. In the real world the hard chairs and complete lack of warm conviviality made me want to leave immediately and fortunately that helped my motivation just then because like gas stations and hotel lobbies at midnight it made you an *outsider* against the *insider*. These places were points of refuge; honorary homes, and they were the only things which separated you from the cold and the night, but not the down and out or insane, because they knew where to go too. These were slightly secret places and were for travellers and motorcyclists like me who had failed to find homes in the ordinary world.

Diary: On the road to Port Hedland

Rode medium hard early on then rode harder. Lots of filming, making me late for everything, but have to document the journey like the chroniclers of old, except the physical has been replaced by the emotional. Ended up at Askuni Roadhouse 268 kms before Port Hedland. Nearly eleven at night, getting tired; stayed in budget cabin accommodation, cottage pie meal. Up at four fifteen to try to make it to Katherine or better still, Daly Waters.

The next day I got up before daylight and rode for miles. I rode with an intensity that belied my modest motorcycle riding skills. I heard the gentle purr of the engine and felt every bump on the narrow wheel-width stretch of tarmac that underpinned me and my bike as we both tried to do this journey, which was not concerned only with time and distance. As I rode my machine between vast acreages of flax and corn, telegraph posts marked my time, peeling past a cramped line of sight as faster and faster I cannoned along the track. It occurred to me as I sat on my bike, my head enclosed in my helmet, how absurd it was to see so much life pass by and so quickly. Why couldn't it be like Aldous Huxley when he walked around his garden without wearing a crash helmet, but under the influence of mescalin, and observed the folds of his trousers and the minutiae of the flora, the detail of which he managed to describe in his book *'The Doors of Perception'*. If you accept that such travel is a state of mind then you could further reduce a journey to the blink of an eye. Riders on certain bikes that sit you so high you can see over hedges might disagree with Huxley. They might say that an afternoon's walk in a garden cannot possibly become the entire subject matter of a book in much the same way that a motorcycle journey around the world in 2 months or 19 riding days can possibly be considered sufficient time to do that properly. *'The Doors of Perception'* became a seminal work. It sold in 100 countries, became an icon of the Beat Generation and inspired the name of the rock group, The Doors. It also gave me hope because this author clearly didn't observe any minimum journey-time as a rule of thumb. Furthermore I reckoned that a flashback should be considered a journey in time even though it takes almost no time for it to happen. It's the ultimate short journey and as with *déjà vu*, it is the closest thing to being ultimately spontaneous. A good journey is like listening to a good joke; when you get it, you don't need to think about it because the understanding of something funny is like a feeling that wells up inside you until, like the appreciation of too much wine or a great adventure, you can't help yourself from laughing, and that also can be something that takes no time at all!

Fitzroy Crossing 05.50; 19th of June.
The aboriginal people hanging around the gas station seemed very gentle and characteristically left me alone to do my own thing. They were used to travellers passing through and watched with quiet indifference. This mirrored the white man's attitude which was equally relaxed. When travellers communicate with locals, there is a difficulty which is in proportion to the amount of time they have. Journeys that involve flying or sailing non stop around the world are in a category that doesn't expect to interact with anyone, other than some global base and then by radio. Such adventures are rare and similar to journeys that move overland very quickly. They had to be the most extreme example of how projects by-pass the natural convention of travel. The usual concept of

going on a journey is related to meeting people. Indigenous peoples are the yardstick for information and local knowledge. They provide the emotional route map for any understanding of the terrain across which you pass. Motorcycling around the world in some record time eliminates all but the most basic precepts of communication. Perhaps for a thousand miles I would say the words, *'please fill my tank up,'* six times, followed by *'thank you'* and maybe *'goodbye'*. I also asked for food intermittently and the following thousand miles would be a variation on this minimalism and might include inquiring about animals on the road. There were exceptions to this but for most of the time there was little opportunity to say to anyone what I had on my mind. I think it needs to be re-emphasised that for days I did not have a single conversation. In any case, if I were to say "My heart is heavy and my soul is slight", most gas station attendants would not know how to respond, so it was best say nothing. Yet truck drivers were almost feverish to tell you how many animals they had wiped out and what hitting one would mean to me. Ultimately, at speed, the only thing you could do was listen.

The lack of meaningful conversation simply emphasised the difference between this journey and most others. It was all extreme; the time away from home, being alone, the speed, the vast distances and a lack of prolonged visibility meant that this journey was also not subjected to the usual rules of social scrutiny. In this respect, it was a project without parallel: you are there, yet not there; materially present but not being; talking yet not conversing; passing through; constantly on the move, alighting only on the forecourts of gas stations to feed and then to move on, and this meant you had no belonging. To stay in that state for a long time causes a social 'micro climate' which alternates between interest and suspicion when people cannot find something with which their own village rules of position and status can identify. Columbus, Pizarro, the conquistadores were thought by the natives to be Gods. When Stanley went in search of Livingstone, he tramped across central Africa with 1800 natives, each carrying boxes which were thought to be the bodies of an army about to be assembled. Now, a traveller's life was not so exotic, especially in the Australian outback. I seemed to qualify barely higher than a vagrant on the social register.

* * * * *

At the turn of the 19th century one of the mightiest of old world adventurers, Alexander von Humbolt, wrote in his diaries that his travels in South America were *'spurred on by an uncertain longing to be transported from a boring daily life to a marvellous world.'* Twelve years earlier, Xavier de Maistre, an inhabitant of Chambery at the foot of the French Alps, created something called 'room-travel' and wrote a book entitled *'Journey around my Bedroom.'* Whereas Humbolt voyaged with ten mules, a sextant, two telescopes, baggage carried by a team of handlers, a theodolite, chronometer, four interpreters and letters of introduction from the King of Spain, de Maistre wore only his pink pyjamas. The boundaries of his travels were not, the *Equinoctial Regions of the New Continent* (as Humbolt entitled his book)*,* but his bed, the sofa, and the edges of his room. It was not until he ventured to the window that he wrote his second volume entitled, *'Nocturnal Expedition around my Bedroom,'* whereby he actually looked out at the night sky. The idea wasn't to disparage the great contemporary journeys; Magellan had found a Western route to the Spice Islands, Drake had sailed around the world; but as de Maistre's brother Joseph observed, room journeys were for those people who had neither spare time nor independent wealth and who were also afraid of the high seas, deep canyons, robberies, periods of loneliness and large crowds; a way of travel particularly suited to anyone who was not rich. In the same way I also wanted to journey as a minimalist. My luggage amounted to a film camera, a credit card and a toothbrush. My transport gave me overland independence from camels and mules and saved me from having to adhere to timetables and places where you hop onto buses and trains. I felt as free as I could be. If it hadn't been for the need to ride so much and so hard each day I would have been freer than a bird.

Once the ride on each continent gets under way, my communication reduces to a smile or some instinctive communion with someone in which words are not needed. Sometimes you check out the toughest member of the group and get him to feel part of the journey that's passing through his patch, and his gang members will fall into line. As long as you don't hang around long enough for a plan to form, even the most dubious characters can understand the unthreatening requirements of someone needing safe conduct through their territory.

I left the gas station at Fitzroy Crossing to ride 288 kilometres and had three hours to get to the one at Halls Creek before it stopped serving. It was essential I didn't miss this fill up because it would have stopped the ride until morning, and that would have cost me eight hours. The deeper into the journey I got, the less time there was to correct any slip in my schedule. The time I had to beat to stand a chance of staying on schedule amounted to 4 days and 15 hours, so eight hours lost now could be a few hundred miles that might not be recaptured later. So finely tuned was the 19 day record that I'd set out to beat, so logistically perfect, that my own inability to compete on such terms meant I had to compensate in different ways. I had to graft more; I also had to take more chances. Three hours later I rushed onto the forecourt as the gas man was beginning to padlock the pumps.

Already behind on the Australian section, there was no choice but to grit my teeth and ride right through the night. The riding hurt me a great deal. During the good moments I felt I was flying, clipping corners en route in such an easy way that little effort was required. A smooth riding action disengaged me from a million wasteful movements and as I rode still and steady it took a long time for me to tire, but when I did, it was hard. I'd never intended to ride so much in the dark, but once again the development of this journey seemed to take on a life of its own. The concentration needed to avoid animals at night exhausted me and I drew from reserves I never knew I had. Wildlife on the road was a consideration for everybody driving at night. Big trucks have been forced into the gutter by hitting large kangaroos. It was much more of a problem for motorcyclists. The risk of serious injury was very high. Truck drivers warned me that the chance of a collision could be as high as 80%. Under exceptional times of drought or when a herd was in the area, they all said to me that a motorcyclist might not get through. A small 'roo would bend the forks, smash a fairing or throw you off the bike; a large one would write it off. A small one would perhaps break your legs, a big mother would kill you. Wombats tense instantly prior to impact and people who have hit them and survived say it's like hitting a boulder. Dead road kill that hasn't been picked clean by the crows will still be fresh and their organs something on which to slip. I have lost count of the number of times I have missed a swollen carcass by inches and a fraction of a second.

Locals reassured me that the recent rains had encouraged the animals not to stray from the interior; that water being plentiful gave them no reason to come to the road to find moisture. Where the water runs from the convex surface of the road to where it joins the dirt, fresh green roots grow and at times of drought animals go there to feed. Outback legend has it that kangaroos commit hara-kiri in front of motorcycles for two reasons; one, the sound of an engine approaching generates the Doppler effect which, when changing in tone from faraway to close-up in a gently smooth logarithmic curve, allows the animal to know precisely where you are, even from a distance of several miles. The moment the rider sees the animal, he brakes, closes down the engine, the sound disperses differently and the animal can no longer track the continuous signal; second, being nocturnal, the animal's vision is adjusted for very low light levels so it is completely blinded by oncoming headlamps. Already in panic he jumps any which way and if there are enough animals, given that there are a variation of four ways to jump, your mortality is reduced to a survival factor of 25%. Statistics show that a person would have to travel on an airline flight every day for 35,000 years to be assured of being in an accident. The survival factor of actually dying from an aeroplane crash is estimated at 82% whilst 100% of all truck drivers told me that in their considerable experience, a motorcyclist hitting a large 'roo has a 100% chance of being killed. Riding at 80 kph I saw two small sets of ears, nothing more, peak out of a perfectly camouflaged landscape and it was certain there would be another hundred nearby, or a thousand, and it reminded me to slow down further.

Collision with an animal is usually fatal on a motorbike but the rains that had started two weeks before my arrival ended a six year drought. Had it not been for that, it would have been impossible to ride at night. I have seen whole herds of kangaroos cross the road and they have a mission to follow whoever is in front. While a broken collar bone would slow this journey down and make it much more difficult, a broken leg would probably end it. There is not much skill in avoiding animals, they jump out in front of you and are suddenly there. All you can do is lower the risk by watching intensely for anything that doesn't look like a bush. A 'roo is so well camouflaged that its dusky colour is practically impossible to detect. By the time you've seen him he's either head first in your fairing or he's gone. If one jumps out, they say, then watch out for the other as they nearly always travel in pairs. If you see a pair, then there are whole moving nomadic townships of animals close by which cannot be seen. Such intensity is exhausting. It's not like a normal night ride where keeping awake is your main consideration. Keeping alive is a major issue as every truck driver has a story of a biker who has succumbed to a 'roo. In time I stopped talking to truckers because you could see they were feeding off the drama. They searched for fear in your eyes and tried to wind their horror stories deep into your psyche until you cracked.

I reached Hall's Creek in time, gassed up and continued immediately to ride the four further hours to Kunnunarra. There, a 24 hour station would allow me to take on fuel until Katherine, another four hours further on and as day prised open the night sky, all the gas stations would then be open for business. At Timber Creek, the plains turned to rolling hills and small-sided canyons. Vast bush was reduced to small dirt brown valleys. In a small settlement nearby I saw a table under a tree and lay down and slept. For two hours I dreamt of nothing; flirted with a few images but remained resolutely asleep without a flicker of anything I could remember, except that when I woke it was still as dark as when I started to sleep and the warm wind was willing me back on the bike. That night I rode with the wind, in fact I was so much part of it the wind and I were old friends. So well was I riding and so fast did I fly, it was easy to conclude that after three days of being in the saddle with just blinks of normal sleep, half of me was dreaming and half of me was awake; the secret was knowing the difference.

Knowing the difference between the parallel journeys of *fastest man* and now was also a check on my reality. It was impossible not to compare the two.

Fastest Man Extract (Stuart Highway 1997)

Each night I camped in the desert, where the day dawns not little by little but suddenly, and it is as hot as noon in an hour. There were no matins of birds in the morning, just rock partridge cocks chuckling over the waterless desolation. There was only the giddy heat on the crown of the head. Flickering shrillness in tingling ears. A subtle glassiness of the sun. Hot sand-blinking eyes. Days upon end drowned in unceasing summer wilderness. More days spent with my thoughts suppurating in the silence and the sun, my life-force gently crisping. I have been to places where trees are so tall that they touch the clouds, so still that all the water from the rains sluices through their leaves and drips on land below that has never been touched by the sun and it is here where the eternal shadows below become so deep that creatures grow big eyes to see. But here the deserts were so vast that they disengaged all notions of reality. Sometimes there was not one single object, tree or rock, on which the eye could focus. Landscapes such as these turn straight lines into circles...Somewhere in the desert I stopped the bike. The wind swooped around me with whispers and caresses. The road smelled of dust and hot stones, all bathed in ancient brooding light, the kind of light you set sail in. The sun began to set and the wind calmed. I climbed up on to the bike and stood on the seat. Higher by four feet, I was suddenly in another world. Wherever I looked I could see flat plains. I imagined I could see the curvature of the earth. I looked over the acacia bushes nearest to the road, and astonishingly, another hundred million came into view. Little bushes that spotted the red clay soil in every direction for as far as could be seen. There was no sound from the engine now and I became aware of how quiet this journey could be.

Carrying on south on the Stuart Highway, little was in my mind except that this was the leg that allowed me to think of Sydney. It was a straight run to Port Augusta and until a little south of Kulgera the route was in the Northern Territories where there was no speed limit and I could really make up some lost time. I grabbed some food at the Poinciana Roadhouse across from the Coles Express station at Hall's Creek and ate a takeaway roast dinner using my seat as my table. I ate this quickly and washed it down with a pint of milk and set off once again into the night. All the next day I rode hard, and the following night at Renner Springs Roadhouse I stopped for a pie as travellers sat chatting cosily in a warm, atmospheric glow. It looked very inviting and a stop at this time of night risked my staying longer than the schedule allowed. Casually asking the chaps at the next table about animals on the road they were predictably laden with doom; "I've lived in these parts all my life and trucked up here more times than I've had hot meals and I tell you you're fucking mad to ride here at night," said a small skinny one.

"That's a bit harsh," said an older one, "I mean, if he's got here he must know what he's doing?"

"Incredibly lucky, but luck don't last forever," said the skinny one again. A third chap who introduced himself as Paul and drove a big truck containing the Australian equivalent of *Nascar* race cars told me he'd just hit a kangaroo and it had forced him off the road.

Mr Skinny was calming down but was still blunt. Because there was a stock pen situated nearby, the 'roos would congregate around that and would spill out into the road. I told them I was listening and it was true, they were beginning to give me cause for real concern. I hadn't slept for 70 odd hours having ridden around 2500 miles and my bag of chips and meat pie was making me sleepy. Paul offered me a bed in his room and suggested I rest until dawn instead of crawling along at 40mph in the dark. In the morning, I could make use of the Territories rule which allowed me to ride as fast as I wanted and make up the time later. Laying all my maps on the floor we all worked out that the route from Port Augustus to Sydney via Broken Hill was 461 kilometres shorter than going on the Hume Highway after Adelaide and Melbourne, so I'd lose less time. It seemed a good plan so I went to Paul's room, showered and slept as soon as my head hit the pillow.

★ ★ ★ ★ ★

Wordsworth thought travelling embellished the soul that a walk across a landscape in some way ennobled our view of life and Pascal was amazed how the small space he occupied was swallowed up in the *infinite immensity of spaces of which he knew nothing and which knew nothing of him.* There is little to compare with the immensity of a desert when standing on a very small boulder looking out over a sea of sand. It is also intoxicating when you then compare human weakness with something so strong and massive that only poetry and biblical similes can adequately describe what you feel and see. While less denuded than a true desert, the bush stretching either side of the Stuart Highway is such a place, and it is only the thin veneer of occasional small towns, perhaps a single building thick, that separate you from a size of nature that reminds you in the most gracious way how much bigger it is than you can possibly imagine it to be.

★ ★ ★ ★ ★

Coobar Pedy

It's about 11.00 am local time. I've ridden since 5 o'clock this morning and am currently in Coober Pedy, which is 550 kms north of Port Augusta on the Stuart Highway . Have almost done 800 miles so far today and am preparing now to ride to Port Augusta, north of Adelaide . From here I will turn east and ride to Broken Hill and on to Sydney. The reason for this change of route is that according to the locals it's a shorter route. Also the alternative route to Melbourne and back up to Sydney passes through lots of speed restricted zones ...schools, hospitals and built-up spaces. A 30-40 kms per hour speed restriction is extremely constricting for me. So instead I will go cross country. In doing that I will lose about 250 miles from my scheduled 5000 miles estimated distance for this stage, but I hope to make that up in a faster time. I am feeling good, and am not too worried about the animals anymore, but I am not being complacent either. The locals tell me that the further south I go, the less chance there is of coming up against kangaroos on the highway. Also, they tell me that there has been a lot of rain last week and apparently that scatters kangaroos from their herd and keeps them far away from the road. This has been a marvelous piece of luck, because it has allowed me to keep up with the schedule. By the time I arrive in Sydney, I should have done approximately 4700 to 4800 miles. Hopefully I'll be an hour or two ahead of the record schedule, and at worst I know I haven't lost any more time.

Halfway down the descent to Port Augusta I stopped at Pimba and sat in Spud's Diner. So tired, I slept with my head on my tank bag. The roaring log fire made me want to stay but half an hour later I left. However, the morning cold catapulted me back into the warmth and finding a table in a corner I tried once again to rest. It was really uncomfortable but I slept for an hour and when I awoke, the sun had pierced the darkness and was a good hour into the sky. I'd forgotten, but it was the mid winter solstice here and the shortest day offered the least favourable riding conditions. I rubbed myself down and shook with an involuntary ripple, rather as a horse might, and in two minutes was out of that door and back on the bike. In a matter of seconds, from a standing start, I was hurtling along at speeds that made road trains look as if they were going backwards.

Twenty kilometres from Port Augustus I took a left turn for the Flinders Range, which were pretty, hillocky and dotted with small farms and streams. On a summer's day you couldn't think of a nicer place to ride but on this winter's day the roads were greasy making the off camber bends treacherous and the rain was bitterly cold. I started this final section to Sydney just after seven in the morning and expected to have to ride cautiously all day. To my surprise and relief, the clouds on the horizon started to break up and soon there was only blue sky. This was something to aim for because I had reconciled myself to having to ride in the rain all the way to Sydney. Eventually my bike and I were bathed in dry, warm light and then a wind started to blow from behind. It was clearly a front of some kind and as I began to ride faster my grip on the accelerator was light as it needed so little response. The wind whipped me along and I raced between fertile winter fields of fresh green grass. Small townships came and went until I stopped at Yunta where I ordered chips and gravy. While I waited for my meal I went to the phone box next to the café and called Trevor in Perth who put me on to the freighters in Sydney. They couldn't help, but they knew people who could, and I soon had my bike booked on a plane from Sydney to Christchurch, New Zealand.

The impetus of the wind and the sun made me think I might gain time on this northerly route; I felt that the decision I'd made to ride here and not further south on the Hume Highway was a true vindication of artistic merit over military-style precision. One way *appeared* to be technically quicker because of the lower population, the other was crammed with schools and housing and the necessary speed restrictions that ensue. The reality was very different.

Just near where I stopped, there was a small store which was like an image from a Norman Rockwell painting, all timber framed surrounded with a picket fence and the evocative sound of rusting hinges squeaking and a tousled-haired boy in awe of my bike. He reminded me of my own boys back home who would run to me when I returned from my travels, the smell of adventure all over me. Here the wind rippled wide puddles across the way and tumbleweed raced across to catch in the bramble. Trees swayed and bent as if never to return and small advertising signposts swung wildly in their frames. Slowly, the weather began to change as the blue sky was wiped black by menacing clouds that threatened rain at any moment. By Broken Hill the wind was chilly and after a brief break to tighten and spray my chain, I put on my waterproof over-suit.

As the sky darkened, the rain began to fall in torrents and to make matters worse the surface of the road deteriorated until my whole body was constantly jarred, even at slow speeds. The suspension on the bike had not been adjusted from the factory settings and, combined with a seat kept purposefully trim for fast track work, it made for a hard ride. Calluses had formed on my backside but having spent much of my life on a racing bicycle, this was something that I was used to. For hours I rode and stopped only to fuel at a gas station where I had my sole conversation of the day. Actually, it wasn't technically a conversation because that requires some verbal exchange between two people and that didn't happen.

An old man was sitting hunched over his dinner of spaghetti rings. It looked disgusting and so did he. Unshaven with deep set eyes and a sunken mouth which appeared to have evolved for the sole purpose of sucking up the juice from his spoon. Suddenly, and without warning, he started to shout, "Shut the fuckin' door, shut it, shut it, *SHUT IT!* it's fuckin' cold yer fuckin' moron!" and pierced me to the core with his stare. So I shut it. There was no way I wanted to discuss customer relations, the Guinness Book of Records or consumer rights because he'd just tell me to fuck off back to the suburbs and wouldn't serve me any petrol, so I did what I was told and hung around until he'd finished. I think the food hit his stomach quickly because he was mellower when he saw that I was being polite and got up without speaking and went out to fill up my tank.

It was still raining and had got colder; the temperature gauge on my bike had stopped moving off its minimum reading. My body didn't feel warm and that made riding more uncomfortable. I had already stuffed my white 'walking trousers' around the top of my neck and back and that helped stop muscle spasms that had begun to form there. When the rain occasionally relented I lifted my visor and my face didn't flinch. In fact, my face had aged greatly; despite my integral helmet and visor, my face seemed to have absorbed all the effort involved in braving the elements; the blistering winds, piercing rains, searing sun, and the freezing cold that can split boulders. All the stress seemed to have set my features in stone. I secretly hoped that the network of extra lines might straighten out after some rest, but right now I looked old. In the mirrors I saw a man with bags under his eyes, cheeks scorched by a freezing breeze, reddened eyelids, piggy, bloodshot eyes and sandstone for skin. It was exactly as it should be. I looked a younger version of that old man at the gas station, but he was riddled with other things and I still had some sparkle left in my eyes whereas his had dulled and he seemed quite mad.

Before Nyangen the lorry drivers got to me again. All they blathered on about were their trucks, where they were heading and the kangaroos that were waiting specifically for me to pass so they could leap out in front of me. After listening to them telling me what an idiot I was riding at night and completely ruining my appetite I sort of 'pulled rank' and told them I'd ridden around Australia and the whole goddamn world six times without ever hitting one. Nevertheless the damage was done and that night I lost my 'bottle'. Up the road I found a caravan site and rented a mobile home for the night. I put the heater on but it gave out more noise than warmth. I didn't wash and barely took off my clothes but climbed quickly into bed and slept.

It was still dark when I rose and I was soon in Dubbo where a policewoman advised me not to ride to Singleton because the roads were closed due to snow. An old lady suggested that I go to Mudgee and through the high hills around Lithgow and Katouba I weaved my weary way on towards Sydney. I had ridden around Australia in a little over four days. I estimated that my time for this stage would be two days faster than when I set my 31 day Guinness world record back in 1997. However I was still six hours behind the time of the couple who set a new motorcycle record in 2002. They'd set the bar very high, although, as a two-up trip, by a different route, it was also a very different adventure and achievement.

Sydney, Australia

Very tired, can't talk, can't think. Rode across from Port Augustus to Sydney via Broken Hill and initially it proved to be an inspired idea - less trucks, well no trucks and the Hume Highway further south carries 3000 a day. Also I and several truck drivers and Jiten in the office worked out that it was 250 miles shorter but this proved not to be the case - I recorded 5030 miles, only 50 miles less than one of the schedules I was following. Until Alice Springs I was on schedule. The second half of my northerly route turned bad - it got dark and the animals were rampant and it turned out to be one of the most dangerous roads I have ever ridden on so had to slow down to less than 40 mph. By daybreak I had ridden nearly 60 hours with only a little sleep - 18 hours sleep since Perth . Filming has taken up more time than it should have done - nearly two hours a day, maybe more, but it is essential as this is what my sponsors are paying for. So many near misses with kangaroos - and just one animal could wipe out this record attempt, maybe even kill me. The truck drivers said that if you were lying in the middle of the road they wouldn't see you. Missed dead animals on the road by a thousandth of a second – animals big enough to crush the front forks. So much to write but so tired. The bike has gone to the freighters already and will be in New Zealand on Saturday. Then the ride starts again, but with less of an animal problem. There will be a small chance of hitting caribou on the Alaska Highway but after that there are no animals on the interstates in the US - this is the only place where I stand a chance of catching up. Am a bit down about being 1000 miles behind the record schedule and left with only 8 or 9 riding days to finishing the circumnavigation. The angels are going to have to stay on my side if I am going to beat this record.

On the flight to New Zealand the Virgin girls on Pacific Blue started giving an aerobics lesson to the few of us on board. "Move your ankles, round and round and then," she paused, "c'mon, get those fingers *twinkle fingers*," and her fingers stretched and closed, "then pull your hands back like Diana Ross *'can't give you love'*," and she jigged and outstretched her arms and back, then held her palms towards all of us in the audience and pulled hard and back on the tips of her fingers. I wasn't a 'twinkle finger' kind of person and sort of dosed, drifting gently around my head for a thought I could lock into. Alienation is always a safe bet when you are alone because when there is no one to tell you how wonderful you are, you need a type of self-belief which I didn't have just at that moment.

Some feelings of alienation are inevitable when you always seem to be sitting alone on the sidewalk, when it's always you who's ordering a table for one while all around you people are enjoying someone else's company. Alienation doesn't have to mean sadness or loneliness but can centre instead on some fracture between the real and the unreal. And what seems real to one person is quite unreal to someone else. Roadhouses, bars and 'planes can give a sense of cosiness but really they are just repositories for strangers. The less intimate the situation the smaller the contrast between feelings of loneliness and that cosy environment because everyone is suffering from some collective anguish. To ride 1100 miles a day around Australia is as unreal to most people as working as a furniture salesman would be to me. Finally the plane landed and I rolled off with the other eight people.

The queue to get through immigration was friendly but slow. I bought a 200ml bottle of Bailey's Irish Cream liqueur and drunk it while I waited. A cloud of suspicion began to hang over me. I was starting to drink and I wondered why. I suppose I was just nervous and drinking calmed me down. A thousand miles behind on a very tight schedule could mean my failing to get the record. I couldn't address this just then, the time just wasn't quite right.

Outside, where the city bus shuttle picks you up, there is a large building with 'United States Antarctic Programme' painted in large letters over the main doors. Further along, there is a greyness that is more than grey, it is the cold colour of winter. The clouds were more than bleak, they were frozen, and there would soon be a frost on the ground. A weak winter sun tried to push through the clouds but instead managed only a pallor of dim light. At least it was dry. The last time I rode here, in 1997, it rained.

High walls separated houses along the road from prying eyes, or invaders. The talk at customs and in the bus was of the rugby. The British Lions were playing the All Blacks and not doing very well. I hadn't even known that they were here. I did care, but as I sat looking out of the window on Fendalton Road, by the large Hagley Park, I was more interested in the leaf-less nakedness of the oaks and the chestnuts. The browning of the fallen leaves was more reminiscent of autumn than winter but the temperature definitely said 'winter'. Apart from the ordinariness, there was not much else to see. When we turned off Harper Avenue onto Park Terrace, boys in football kit reminded me again of my own little lads who would be camping with their mum. It's only when you see such things that you make those connections and when you're in the Antipodes, you know you're a very long way from home.

After the browning chestnuts, we reached Gloucester Street and the wavy glass building of the art gallery where the bus turned right past the Café Roma and left onto Worcester Street before turning into Cathedral Square, where I got off. Everything was quieter than usual and Christchurch isn't a city like Sydney anyway – it's more of a large town. The usual tinny clatter of life marching on bone-dry earth was replaced by a duller sound in the cold.

I went into the main tourist and visitor centre on the square and checked out the ferry times across the Cook Strait. Money was getting tight so I booked into the Thomas 'Hotel' in Hereford Street, which was really more of a back-packers' hostel. After paying 22 dollars – about £8 - for a bunk bed with linen, I left a deposit for the key and carried on with my jobs. There was a large internet facility on the corner of the square called *Blah Blah* so I responded to a couple of emails, bought myself a phone card to call my children and settled down with a glass of wine in a bistro to write before spending the evening at the cinema. These little 'mind treats' keep you from wanting to get the next flight home. I had been away from my family for weeks now and was starting to suffer from profound homesickness. I knew from the early days of my travelling that when this happens I am like a ferret being torched from a hole and just hope the direction I'm going is homeward, otherwise I get burnt.

The city was crawling with sad Brits who'd just seen the Lions thrashed by the All Blacks. The match result was so poor it was embarrassing. You could feel the despondency in the air and beer was being sold by the tanker-load as the British fans tried to drown their sorrows. Hundreds of people, all dressed in Lions' colours, had taken a year's holiday time and shelled out months of pay only to see their team humiliated. The next test in Wellington would decide whether they would have done better to stay at home and spend their money on new conservatories.

I sat at the bar of a bistro on Oxford Terrace and drank my two glasses of wine. Apart from the Bailey's at the airport earlier in the day it was the first alcohol that had crossed my lips in weeks. I dared not drink more. If I did I would walk in a straight line across the city, across to the horizon and into the mountains until the alcohol wore off. After such a technical expedition, where so much paperwork accompanied the exercise, I needed a simple journey in my soul. The wine would have convinced me that to walk in a straight line until sober was as simple as it gets. Worse still, if I had the pouch of cheese my father always took on his fantasies into the forest, along with a never-ending flask of wine, I would have gone further until I came to the sea. At such times there is a tempest that breaks free from the heart which everyone knows has a power to change people's lives. Everyone could be the person in their dreams, but isn't that like trying to travel at the speed of light? The closer you get to knowing yourself, the harder it becomes, until, right at the very point of enlightenment, everything stops.

It was hard to know about these things. At the end of every day and night, I was just a motorcyclist going around the world very fast, and just then I didn't need to know any more. Propping up the bar I was invisible. Just a man writing, sipping his second glass of wine, no trouble to anyone, begging himself not to drink more because it was awfully cold out there. The mountains beckoned − it was like looking over the edge of a cliff. I felt seduced, sighed and capitulated and drank a third glass of wine. This was getting dangerous. No more wine tonight. 'Get this journey over', I said to myself quietly 'and then tack across to the sea, but not now'.

Christchurch, New Zealand

Just arrived. The bike arrives today and tomorrow I will try to get it out of customs. Just checked the ferries across the Cook Strait − 3 a day. I need to co-ordinate these with a quick release for the bike and also to avoid any possibility of snow. It is colder here − freezing temperatures at night. I am going to see if customs are 24 hours - they usually are - and will release the bike at 05.00. They may respond to this request and do me a favour so I don't have to ride across the North Island desert road at night. We will see. New Zealand is much quieter than Australia. The British Lions are here barely afloat, *just my face above the surface of the water. I don't know why I didn't sink, maybe it just wasn't my time to die. After sailing across Europe and the Channel, I was back in London, passing under Tower Bridge, and in a blur, ended up travelling north along the Grand Union Canal in Northamptonshire. I had nothing left when I returned to England. Mentally I was shot to bits. I just wanted everything to end so I could hide away and rest. My Professor girlfriend had chucked me. Yep, I was well and truly fucked. And then I met Hennie.*

I still had no money, prospects were untidy and there I was with this girl who wouldn't tell me her family name, and whom I fell in love with at first sight. Of course it couldn't last. I didn't know it then, but a rabbit has more chance of mating with a moose than she had of seeing me into old age but I didn't care and asked her to marry me anyway."

The 650 miles to Auckland was very important but it was essentially a linking part of the project, connecting the 5000 mile journey around Australia to the 7000 mile ride around North America. In one sense, the whole thing was ridiculous. Its meaning would soon be fossilised into some abyss of forgetfulness. Some poet or wit would have it relegated to stupidity before the ink was dry. Did I care? Of course not. From where I was, it was easy to imagine that no one would be interested in this event for any longer than the time it took to read about it in the papers, if it even got in them. And I expected the number of days to be miscalculated and my name to be spelt incorrectly. Apart from a few family members and friends and some genuine, enlightened *others*, it was a fair bet that no one gave a fuck. Except, I did.

I wanted to be the Fastest Man around the World again. Very few people have worked hard enough to have won that title and I wanted it back so badly; if it weren't for the kids, then, poor fool, I would gladly die for the privilege. You have think in this perverse way to even make the achievement

and the English and Irish fans are being made very welcome - but apparently we got thrashed so spirits are low. I am also feeling very homesick. The trip is taking its toll. It is impossible to ride 18 or 19 days around the world, it obviously takes longer with the shipping and that is what takes the nerve but it is so much harder alone - week after week I have to sort everything over here myself. No one to talk to. I mean it's not that bad but I miss my family and my kids. This record is important to me, so important to me. I want so badly to be the fastest Man Around the World again - and I will. I am psyching myself up to do the ride of my life in the USA to snatch it back. I will try my hardest. If I fail it will be the second biggest failure of my life and I don't want any more failures - I have sacrificed too much to fail. I will not fail.

The next day I called the freighter's office in Auckland and spoke to Steve on his mobile. He put me onto Tony who was the handling agent for my consignment in Christchurch.

"Where are you now mate?"

"In a phone box,"

"Can you see anything?"

"The *Dux Lux* pub,"

"Know it, hang on," and I could hear him having another conversation on his other phone, "be there in a *jif*," he said, "give the boy your carnet and we'll get your bike out either tomorrow or break of day the next," and rang off. Surprised at his incredible efficiency, I had barely put the receiver down when a bicycle courier arrived that moment and took the document off me to be delivered to Tony for clearance. That left the way free for a quick look around before an evening with a major passion of my life, the cinema.

Going to the movies has saved me from myself in so many places. *Cinema Paradiso* in Perth offers the most delicious post-festival art films while Sydney and New York do everything. Broome does open air cinema while Singapore usually only does mainstream and with rare exceptions, is as cinematically experimental as nasal spray. Cairo shows big screen and provides *chai*; tea-sellers offer the drink throughout the performance, chinking their trays and handing out little clay cups or glasses steaming with tea, roasted almost, in cinnamon.

Conveniently situated opposite my digs, Christchurch has an arts centre which houses three movie theatres and I was booked in for two films that night, one of which, *The Light*, was a film about a community centred around an isolated lighthouse in Brittany. The other film, *Dear Frankie*, was about a nine year-old deaf boy, Frankie, and his single mum Lizzie who have been on the move ever since Frankie can remember, most recently arriving in a seaside Scottish town. Wanting to protect her son from the truth that they've run away from his father, Lizzie invents a story that he was away at sea on the HMS Accra. Every few weeks, Lizzie writes a make-believe letter to Frankie, supposedly from his father, telling of his adventures in exotic lands. A movie was a rare treat. Afterwards I went to *Le Café*, a back stage wine bar, and sat in a gallery above the diners below.

This may sound odd, but on a round-the-world journey, too much stimulation can mean that you don't notice very much and remember less. One desert starts to resemble another and when you compare the sublime magnificence of a particular view with another, their incredibleness is sometimes seen through a foggy lens and is quickly forgotten.

Filming my journey had compromised the attempt to break the record, easily costing me 30 hours, but it was an essential portfolio of images. They may or may not have relevance in a world which is addicted to speed yet is somehow dislocated from the human effort needed to achieve it. Journeys like this are overlooked by people of a certain mind-set who think that everything has already been done. Given the amount of time

we're likely to inhabit the earth, it's sad that some peopl
there is nothing new left to do. With this in mind I succ
to a bottle of wine, my spirit weakened by the effort of
to do something new against a backdrop of indifference
an increasingly strong desire to go home coupled with a
of intellectual depression. The scent of my sons and dau
was now inside me, and in those circumstances it
willpower of epic proportions not to just return an
damned. So I drank a little more. I drank a red wine
claimed to be best drunk *'alfresco, under clear blue skies*
weeping willows were to sway gently in the summer breeze'. I d
need this alcohol, but it did help me address the questio
the penultimate stage and quite why I was here.

I thought back to the time when the demon drink nearly ~~~~
for me, when I jumped into the Danube during a hugely successful trip with two canal boats from England to the Black Sea which had monumentally disastrous moments. I related it in my 2004 book 'Loneliness of the Long Distance Biker', last year.

> *"It had been a hard journey down the Danube. I'd sunk one of the*
> *boats in 80mph winds, nearly drowned, lost everything, craned it*
> *back up and started again four days later. I'd sailed past Vukovar in*
> *Serbia just after the atrocious bombing, and on the way home, hitch*
> *hiked with my 20 tons of rusting steel 3000 miles back to German*
> *attached to a Romanian push tug called Issacci 9. When I jump*
> *into the Danube fully clothed, I was so drunk I couldn't think*
> *was at Regensburg, where I'd moored my own boats by the lock,*
> *had been invited to party on a passing cruise boat. I got bored*
> *the company and jumped overboard. I don't remember being*
> *in a German prison but I do remember the thumping of propell*
> *feet from where I floated, before the river was closed to shippin*
> *soon unconscious and drifted downstream for 20 kilometre*
> *was picked up. And why was I in such a state? I had beer*
> *and I had gone mad. For an hour or more I drifted i*

possible. Your heart has to cry to the point it might burst; your brain must be prepared to explode. Everything has to be set aside for that brief time in your life when nothing matters more than this task in hand. That's what separates those who think about it from those who do it. There is a point where the senses can become debilitated, after which only the few survive, or want to. Guardian Angels can thrust you back to normality, but it's no secret that such an odyssey can send you off kilter. As I sat in a restaurant somewhere in Christchurch on the other side of the world just a few hours away from my own antipodes, I felt like a general about to make a charge. I didn't have the lines of cavalrymen and horses in blinkers and infantry running behind but in my own small way, it felt rather like that. How can you engage in the end game with reason? This kind of madness drives you to search for something that is not there, for isn't that what discovery is all about? I knew that there was no justification for such a journey as this, because this was a journey without reason.

Christchurch, New Zealand

Waiting on a call from the air freighters here in Christchurch – hope to get the news I can have the bike first thing in the morning. Today is a beautiful and sunny day, not warm, but no snow. I will feel better when I am on the bike - the bike to me has become my home or at least my only interface with the world. I think that most bikers feel this way after a while riding, but when you do something as extreme as this it emphasises this much more. The home sickness hasn't really left me. I am now anxious to get on my way before the rot sets in and I cut and run and just head for home! I wouldn't do that but it does illustrate the pull from home when you get into your head that you areactually on your way home. Instead, the North American section could become the hardest section so far, especially in terms of miles ridden. The wildlife issue doesn't really worry me, although the caribou on the Alaskan Highway will be there at night,

145

but it is the pressure of knowing I have to ride at least 1200 miles a day if I am to get this record. There is no chance of a slip up, I cannot make up any more lost time. Every day's target must be met. I will be less nervous when I get started.

Still waiting for the bike

It's at times like this that you have to be at your most composed. The stop / start nature of this event is very hard. You have to 'psych' yourself up to a very high level of skilful riding across distances that most riders would never wish to ride. You then have to stop and become quiet again. In a sense you steady yourself for the next phase, but you also lose momentum badly. Psychologically it is very hard because the rush of energy and dynamic movement is replaced by nothing and you have to fill the vacuum. Insecurities and uncertainties pop into your head - the usual stuff such as, Why do it? Who cares? etc. That is not the important issue because who cares what anyone of us does - be it at work or at home? And yet, I believe that people do. I am inspired by all sorts of people and learn from that, and God knows, I still need a lot of learning. I also hope that just a few people are inspired by this journey. Not simply the riding, but also the never-ending perseverance. I might emphasise the difficulties of missing kangaroos over missing my family, but both are incredibly hard. A journey like this can be compared to being on tour - or anything that takes you away from home - and not everyone can cope with it. My own little family can; well, the children can because this is all they have known. My wife decided she'd had enough, and that is her own fine decision for her. So when you lose someone very important to you, you begin to realise that events like this really do have worth, they have to, otherwise you lose everything. Belief in yourself, even when sometimes there doesn't seem to be much to believe in seems to be what it's all about.

A few hours later

The bike has passed its customs inspection and I am just waiting for the paperwork to be signed off. I can have it very late tonight or first thing in the morning, so I'm going to take the second option. Even this little section of 650 miles can't be underestimated. I'm not anticipating gaining any time but expect to meet the 10.00am ferry across the Cook Strait which docks around two and half hours later *which means I can cross the middle desert plateau road to Auckland during the day. This will make a change as half of my journey so far has been ridden at night. It's getting harder and harder to keep re-starting this journey but not far to go now. The freighting to Anchorage is being booked and this should happen fairly fluidly once I get to the North Island. The service for the bike has already been booked in Don's Motorcycle Shop in Anchorage where we have allowed his mechanics one hour to change the tyres, drop the oil and change the oil and air filters and possibly look at the chain and sprockets. I'm beginning to detect a tight spot in my chain so maybe it should be looked at. A mechanical failing at this stage would be a disaster.*

A few more hours later

I leave Christchurch at 05.00 Wednesday morning. Customs clearance with the freighters is 24 hours and allows me to leave first thing in the morning. Then I can film the journey up to Auckland. I have 15 hours to cover the 1000 kms. I feel a bit nervous but that is a good thing – I have been feeling down but hopefully will recover during the ride; I usually do. I know myself very well and I have to go through a process. When I come out the other side I will be fighting fit. Everything is set for the final showdown in the US. Normally I am more than capable of riding 24 hours a day and once I've got the first day out of the way down the Alaskan Highway I will be fine. I appreciate all the support from back home that I'm getting - thanks to everyone. The film is beginning to take shape too. Will write again from Auckland.

The next day I left for Auckland. Distance: 1000 kilometres, time to beat, around 16 hours. By Kaikora the sun began to rise. The black curtain of night was slowly pulled apart. I sat in the only café that was open and ate a pie for breakfast followed by a cup of tea. Such a small thing for me to do had become a luxury. I'd begun to notice how little free time I now had. After Kaikora I rode hard to Picton and was early for the departure of the ferry so lay down beside my bike at the head of the queue of cars and slept until the ticket collector woke me to tell me to board. The ship was leaving 30 minutes late and that was bad news – it was time I would have to make up from somewhere. I was unsure whether or not the official record clock stopped on this occasion and presumed that it didn't. On the boat I slept some more. When it docked I continued north through a wintery landscape. I had no time to write or film and large parts of New Zealand passed like a beautiful dream that you can't quite remember. I rode down to Wanganui until I realised I had gone the wrong way. I had been thinking about my family for 150 kilometres and was hopelessly lost and had to go back the way I'd come.

By the time I got to Auckland I had lost another three hours on my planned schedule for this part of the world. In passing Wellington I had at least fulfilled another technical requirement of this record attempt, since it was the antipodal point to Madrid. Immediately I found my air freighters and had my bike packaged before flying out to Los Angeles where I had 24 hours break before flying north to Anchorage.

In Auckland, New Zealand
Just got into Auckland, over 1000 kilometres from Christchurch. The time taken would have been 15 hours 45 minutes but ended up being 17 hours and 15 minutes due to me taking a wrong turn in the dark and being convinced I was going north, when for 120 km on a very windy road I was going south west. Really annoying, but I had to laugh. I am actually riding more strongly again. The lack of any animals on the road gives me more confidence to push hard, although last night there was black ice on many stretches and all you can do is ride upright and not brake and it seemed to work.

The bike has developed a rumble at high speed and I think it's either a tight spot on the chain or a valve, or even the tyres, as they are virtually flat. The tyres, incidentally, are Continental Road Attacks. They've done 6000 miles and the back is OK for another 500, while the front is easily good for another 1000. And that's on hard, rough quartz-embedded tarmac. And they still grip well.

Meanwhile, the bike is now packed for shipment and I fly to Anchorage tomorrow with a stopover in Los Angeles. I feel tired but am in great health and getting ready for the last week when I plan to ride 1350+ miles a day - mostly because I just want to get home, as well as get the record. This whole event is as much to do with patience as it is to do with speed.

Got some great film, this could be a good movie; we shall see. Must have done 12,000 miles or so in about 12 days; I think we can improve on this. The bike arrives in Alaska on Tuesday - the only freight flight we could get.

LOS ANGELES

The location of the hostel was next to Muscle Beach, a small fenced off area where beef cake men exercised their huge muscles wearing the tightest of lycra underpants in full view of everyone walking by. It was easy to see that for them, this exhibitionism was what gave meaning to their lives. The way they strutted to the various pieces of gymnastic equipment could have won an Oscar and looking at their outrageously defined musculature, it was clearly a whole way of life. Several were completely covered in poorly etched tattoos, like Robert de Niro in the film *Cape Fear*. They had an attitude which made them all look as if they had done twenty years in prison for murder and had marked time by scratching every day on their body with a compass and a biro.

Standing by a food hatch where slices of dog-eared pizza were served for a dollar, I had reached a point in the journey where I was starting to question the whole concept of what I was doing. It wasn't that I didn't like being here, it was just that I now wanted to be somewhere else. Homesick, and longing to rest, I just wanted to be with my friends and family back home but was forcing myself to finish this Herculean task that I'd set myself, one which I knew some people would consider pointless. A mathematician, for example, might think of me as the motorcycling equivalent of a *muscleman*, operating my bike repetitiously just as I had done many times before, and for no good reason. My dad, sitting in the pub in heaven, would still think everything I did was wonderful. My friends questioned the need to do it again and my kids had begun to miss me and to get their countries mixed up. To their mother it was a threat to the family unit and she had no more than a passing sulky interest. People who didn't know me gave notional support but still asked the simple question: '*Why?*' Certainly it made money, and everyone in the world surely empathised with that; after all, the repetition of meaningless tasks is usually linked to having to earn money to live. So, there was a financial sense to it at least but I was still trying to work out whether there was any deeper philosophical meaning to riding a motorcycle around the world.

In Venice Beach, Los Angeles – between flights.

I've arrived at the famous Venice Beach (White Men Don't Play Basketball) and also close to Muscle Beach where people work out. It certainly is a strange place but friendly enough. The bike is being made ready to fly to Anchorage and I fly up to Alaska tomorrow on the 07.00 flight. I am now accustomed to the stop-start nature of this project and this will be reflected in the film. At this stage, it's hard to know how the film will look but it is the only representation of what a fast journey around the world is like because no one else has done it. Most people have got more sense than to be a world blogger when there are more interesting things to turn your attention to. So for what it's worth, as I write my diary, mostly to myself, I am really deeply homesick for family and home. I suppose that this is a state of mind which I have learnt to overcome. When I get back I imagine I'll want to be away again but that's always the way, isn't it? I'll be grounded with the family for several weeks before I take twelve riders to the Iranian border with my mate Marco. A few days after that I'll be taking twenty riders around the Coast of Britain after which I take more riders to Morocco.

A service for the R1 has been booked at Don's Motorcycle Shop in Anchorage as the bike has developed a low-level rumble at about 6000 revs in top. The bike must be in the best shape possible to cope with the final big stage as I have to ride over 1250 miles each day; on US freeways that is perfectly feasible.

The weather here is foggy and cool, not sunny and with the possibility of rain. Right now, Venice Beach is waking up and vendors are putting out their chairs. Los Angeles is so spread out that it's more like a county than a city. Hollywood is in LA, but it's a two hour ride from here, which is the time it takes me to get from South Wales to London.

The bike was still in Auckland and my freighting agent was trying to get the dangerous goods certification organised. If this were to happen as I left then it would be flown to Anchorage the next day to arrive about the same time as me. My airline booker in Christchurch could get me to LA, but couldn't get me to Anchorage for 48 hours. Money was tight and I'd thought of camping out at the airport when I noticed adverts for a backpacker's hostel at Venice Beach, which at $30 for the night was affordable. Once I called them, they sent a shuttle bus to collect me and by mid afternoon I was fast asleep on my bunk.

If there is a place in America that shows how people find meaning in what they do it is on Venice Beach. Everyone has a role, from the druggies to the boys playing basketball: from the tarot card readers and the artists, to the musicians, cyclists and skateboarders, food makers and drink dispensers; it has all become part of a linear circus along the boardwalk between here and Santa Monica. Even the winos celebrate their addiction in song and try to earn money for their next drink.

I was in a strange mood. I'd slept all afternoon. For a dollar I could eat fried sliced potatoes smothered in ketchup which was enough to assuage my hunger after which I went for a coffee opposite my hostel at a French café called the Café des Plages. Just across the market square before the boardwalk and the sea, several marquees and a stage had been built. Something to do with inaugurating a councillor. I stood next to the mayor of Los Angeles, a small and friendly Hispanic chap called Villaraisagosa, while I drank free bottled water. There were also free Danish pastries and the LA Freedom Band trumpeted the great and good into position for the breathless, self-congratulatory speeches. Afterwards I hung back in the Café des Plages listening to Madonna. If ever a pop icon suited the area it was her. There was something expensively trashy about this part of town, the second most visited place in California after Disneyland.

The Café was decorated in light, washed, beach colours with doors hand painted in Mediterranean blue. The coffee, while not strong was freshly pressed and hot and I could sit quietly without anyone bothering me. So afraid are Americans of getting their heads blown away by some freak they are conspicuously polite, especially if you are sufficiently different to give off ambiguous signals. A little eccentricity might not get you an invitation to their home but it keeps repetitious questions at bay. I sat in the café fairly glumly watching the coupés and cabriolets drive slowly past on the way to the beach. It was a Saturday and the waitress, who had spent some time in London, allowed me to stay even though I wasn't eating. Outside it was getting hot, but here, the coolness let me write more comfortably. The small road junction was full of cars. The run-down College Café stood opposite, an even dingier hostel was situated next door and further down the side street to the beach a tattoo parlour lay empty. I was sinking into a mindset of homesickness on a level I hadn't experienced since cycling back from faraway to see my dad. Homesickness, like lovesickness, is an illness which, once diagnosed, needs treating. At that moment, if I'd had the money, I would have flown home. I felt my time on the road had come to an end and that I was a week too late to finish off the journey. I hoped the morning would change my mind.

For a long time I have thought that much of what I've done has been of no importance. However, I took some solace from the thought that what I do is not much more or less meaningless than what a lot of other people do. The idea of writing a report to give to y, sanctioned by z which is either implemented or shredded, gave me the horrors. The army of bureaucrats that makes up the vast stratum of middle management accounted for millions of people's lives, and much of that way of life would be passed on to their unfortunate progeny, but it was too grey for me. Yet here I was, trying to ride over 2000 kilometres each day, putting my life at risk and leaving my family to fend for itself; where was the glory in that, the bureaucrats would ask. I got up, paid and decided to lie down for a while. My reserves of energy had diminished quickly and I now felt tired after little effort.

The next day I called the freighting agent in New Zealand and found that the bike was on its way. I too would be leaving for Anchorage later and had a little time to relax on the beach before catching my flight.

Anchorage

I so didn't want to be here. I'm in Anchorage. Just flown in from LA. Jumped on the bus to downtown and when I got to the hostel off G Street and 4th it was closed. A guy there gave me an address in the suburbs for a cheap house to stay and told me to get the 13 or 45 to get to the edge of town. The driver on the 13 dropped me off after one stop telling me I needed number 45 and said that if I told the next driver that I'd already paid Rick, then I wouldn't have to pay again.

There's nothing wrong with Anchorage but my head was in the wrong space. Because I had to wait for the bike from Auckland - it might take three days but could take five, depending on whether Janine managed to get the men handling the Dangerous Goods certificate out on a Friday. I knew I needed all my reserves of patience to get through this one. I felt more at home when I was stuck in India, and it was a lot cheaper. Alaska is the most expensive state in the US and my funds were low - ten dollars cash in my pocket, three or four hundred on my card. The journey had cost more than I'd budgeted for because it had taken longer. The record concept was far from my head just then and I decided that when I got on my bike again I was going to ride until I dropped. I wanted the record, badly; I wanted to see my kids more. I was finding it hard to be away any longer.

I needed to eat, that would make me feel better. I'd only had a small sandwich and a bun since LA. I was beginning to constantly watch the cost of things. I felt emotionally and creatively dry. When you are on the road you are sometimes in a desert.

The bus ride into town took half an hour and the number 45 out of town was supposed to take me to my accommodation and should have taken 20 minutes but the driver forgot I was on the bus so had to drop me off on the way back. Hardly Shackleton stuck on an ice floe, but tiresome nevertheless. When I arrived at the house I walked around it and nearly went back into town, when a friendly guy came up to me and said he'd been waiting at the bus stop. He said that the bus company had called through and said I was on my way and would he watch out for me. Inside I was introduced to a medium sized man with a largish belly who introduced himself as Tim and then sat down quietly to see what it was all about. Another guy, maybe Haitian, came in and didn't say hello. Tim looked all American with his shaven head while another guy came in who looked almost native with dark skin and was the first to get up and shake my hand. The Haitian guy left and didn't seem too friendly and for a while I said nothing then excused myself and went to buy some groceries from nearby.

I spoke to the big guy at the gas station on the corner and when I asked him what the neighbourhood was like he said it was a ghetto. He said it was the worst district of the city, full of crack heads and prostitutes who would come out at night. "Every house here sells drugs," he said, "but you'll be OK, you're safe at least during the day." The big guy spoke in a quiet falsetto voice and had an urgent, nervous camp-ness about him, as if he was expecting to be ravaged by lions at any moment. I thanked him for his information and he directed me to where I could collect my provisions, two blocks down the highway on the right. There I bought potatoes, tomatoes, an onion, some bread and milk and a packet of bacon. When I got back I made a point of introducing myself to the Haitian-looking guy who turned out to be half Puerto Rican on his mum's side; she lived in New York. He beamed and said "Marcus," as he shook my hand. He was sitting with a nice looking girl wearing pink lipstick and matching pink shoes and hat; "this is my ex wife," he said. She was lovely, and of German Japanese origin. She was in the process of breaking up with her Dominican Republic boyfriend and apparently going back to her Puerto Rican ex-husband. "I want that," he said, and she seemed quite responsive to his attentions. I told him that he was a lucky man and I knew he'd like that because everyone likes to think of themselves as being *lucky*. When she left he started talking about himself, about how she had helped him change and show him love and help him have less tantrums and be less egocentric and how he had overcome his addictions. I didn't need to know more and guessed the rest. To me, he was just a nice guy. When I offered to make something to eat, the guy whose name I forgot offered his eggs and I set to work in the kitchen.

Tim sat all day at his computer playing some card game. He talked about the time he was in Hawaii and how he was going to buy a car someday. Quiet, with a dry humour, he was also a nice chap and when I asked him what he was going to do he said that being up here was an experiment. I imagined that every one of these men had enjoyed many experiments in their lives because I think it's true that anyone who ends up here is like the laboratory rat who found the door of his cage somehow unlocked and took his chance to escape. "I mean it's pretty expensive to eat out here ya know," said Tim suddenly opening up, "I mean for $3 I can eat all I want and not finish in Michigan, but here for $8, I'm still hungry, and there the girls wear bikinis,"

"Why, is it sunny there?" I said,

"Heck no," he said, looking at me as if I was stupid, "they're there to attract the men from the factory see. I mean here you've got the little *titty* bars but the beer is darn expensive; down the road you've got *Hooters* and they've some fine looking girls but ya can't afford to go." Tim was on a tight budget and so was his conversation. None of the guys in the house had much money but they dealt with it well. By midnight, it was still light, which was great news for me. It meant I would be able to ride all night as if it were day, but now it was time for bed.

Next morning when I awoke, Marcus was already sitting up, smoking in his bunk. He politely asked me if I minded but carried on anyway. This hostel wasn't a normal backpacking place; it was more like a private house with long term locals paying rent. Some worked and some didn't. Occasionally backpackers turned up mistaking it for a conventional youth hostel, but Tim said it was rare. "There was once a saucy chick from Finland, she was really slutty, just how I like 'em, and there were a few people from Bulgaria or somewhere once," he said, "but people like that don't come often." While I was there, two girls turned up to look around and somehow I knew they wouldn't come back. Too many men. It was odd how well I immediately fitted in. Marcus had gone back to sleep which was one way to keep your costs down. I got up, washed and shaved. I quite liked the guys and because I'd made a big effort to fit in they liked me. As a traveller passing through, if you stay quiet and listen carefully you get to hear the stories from other men's souls.

There are only a few people I can talk to and *R* and I chatted on the phone about the difficulties of being an adventurer. It was hard on everyone, me, my family and even my friends found access to me difficult. I told *R* that I was trying to express myself, trying to explain what *meaning* a project like this had and wondering whether there were resonances with life in general; whether other people could empathise with the long distance and the emotional demands. A week or two earlier *R* had sent me a quote from Byron which showed how hard it was for him to articulate his own feelings. I hadn't time to think about it then so later, after our conversation, I went back into my emails and re-examined it.

★ ★ ★ ★ ★

There is a small mountain near where I live called Cader Idris. They say that if you climb to the top and stay overnight you return the next day either a poet or a madman. It is the most sacred mountain in Wales. I said to *R* that if you wrote something about it while you were there, by the cwms and corries, standing next to the dark slate, then this must give a different pulse from what you might feel later when you got back, sipping wine in your comfortable house. The content and the quality of the writing would be different, surely changing *in situ* to infuse a more formidable substance in the text. It is perhaps more in context, in time and place, and we discussed how that must create more immediacy, maybe thoughts that were more raw. It was the same anywhere you happened to be and it was in Mountain View where I drew reference that day.

Another person came into the room, a coloured man who acknowledged me and sat down on the sofa and watched the TV with everyone else. After a while he started talking, telling a story, and it was impossible for me not to listen because it was a story worth hearing.

"I was in San Diego and they fingered me and took me to some underground *goddamn* basement and they take the cuffs off me and I was just sitting there and the *mother-son-of-a-bitch* left me there, and he said *'I've seen you down the highway and I know you've got drugs'* and I said *'no way man, I'm clean man, I'm just not dirty'* and it was true, I had nothing."

There was a pause and from the way Marcus listened and asked questions it was clearly a story that hadn't been told here before. "I've sold so much dope in my time I can tell you. I was worth $300 000 that night and could've made a million. And every Friday, (you know we get paid on Thursday night, and we get our cheques cashed), and in 30 minutes I sold cookies the size and thickness of that saucer and I was cleaned out. I tell you, in 30 minutes I was good. In the state of Texas I was there in the early '80s, playing pool, shooting draughts. Between the craps and the cards my hustle was pool." He paused briefly while the men compared notes on their pool before he continued, "Meanwhile I met this brother named Billie Ray and he was shooting with one hand with diamonds on his fingers like you've never seen and I stood there watching for a while and he called me over. I called him *Goldfinger*, but you know he can't beat me with one hand man and I beat him. Anyway, so we chatted and he said "Let's play some craps" and the next day I saw this was a hustle and the devil's on my side so this brother, who was a pimp, but I don't know any pimps, I don't know nothing like this, but he had women, black and white, and he was into a whole lotta shit and I got three years probation."

"Is he still kicking?" Marcus had spent most of his time listening before interrupting.

"Oh yeah, he had a little gay strip somewhere, yeah, he's still kicking."

"I know the guy you're talking about," said Tim, "or if it wasn't him it was a close associate. He was in Hawaii in a shitty restaurant. He was the one who disposed of Jimmy Hoffa's body parts when he was 19. He also said he'd had dinner with Princess Di and I said to him that if you tell lies, at least tell believable ones." The black guy's monologue suddenly ran out of steam and Tim got up to make some lunch. After that he left to have a smoke on the porch. Marcus had either left the house or was back in bed, I didn't know. The black guy was watching a violent prison movie on the TV. When I realised the main character was Van Damme who had just killed the baddest man in the prison, Marcus suddenly looked over my shoulder and said, "it's like that, I can tell you. You kill the biggest dude and the line opens up for you."

It was sunny outside, the sound of several police sirens came and stopped not far away and it seemed a good time for a walk. When I got back I started chatting with the coloured guy who said he was called Joe but I made a mental note to call him somebody else when I wrote up his story. It had something to do with protecting the guilty pretending to be innocent, but it felt more like the innocent trying to make himself sound more impressive; he was really a welder and had been for the past 30 years and there's only so much you can say about that. He said that once, he drove from Texas to San Francisco in 20 hours, just fuelling and riding, went to see his uncle, a card sharp in the city who ran his own thing. When I asked him why he was here in Anchorage, (just being friendly and just wanting to build his character), a flash of defensiveness crossed his face before he instantly recovered. "Well I live here, and my wife doesn't want me to live at home no more, and you know, everyone has his problems in every country." I told him that my wife had kind of done the same. This conversation seemed to reverberate throughout all of these men's hearts; you could see they all carried the same kind of pain. "Hell, that's right, your wife kicked you out and you go round the world; *ferck,* that's the way to do it. Hey Tim, I'm going around the world on a *m-o-t-o-r-c-y-c-l-e,*" and turned to drink his beer.

"So what is this, is it yer notes on yer journey or what?" Tim had wandered up to me on the way to the porch for another smoke.

"Well sort of, it is a diary and I've just been reading about a Greek myth brought up to date by the French existentialist philosopher Albert Camus and I'm trying to incorporate that into my writing."

"Huh, sounds good, how many pages?"

"I don't know," I said, "about as thick as that," and showed him a few pages out of the telephone directory which indicated a thin book. That didn't seem to impress him and he wandered off back to the TV. American wrestling had been on all night and the fake posturing was tedious and when Marcus walked in he just called it '*shit-ass fake garbage*' and said he'd get it off soon enough.

"So," said Tim, looking back over his shoulder at me, "What exactly are you writing?" I think he suspected me of listening in to their conversations and of course he was quite right.

"I'm kind of talking to myself," I replied, "sort of in my head".

"Do it all the time," he said, "everyone does,"

"But not with some imaginary made-up individual that you've given a name to?"

"Sure, why not?" he said quite generously. "We're all a bit cuckoo in our own way you know, it's just that some of us are better at hiding it than others." And he turned back to the TV. 'Phew', I thought to myself, 'that was a close call,' and I carried on with my writing.

"Do you think what you do is worthwhile?" said The Interviewer.

"Well, if I assume I was stupid enough to think it wasn't and then still do it that makes me absurd?" I said.

"Let me prove that for you."

Thanks. I was nervous that he would see things in my journey, or rather see emptiness's and voids that I hadn't recognised. Part of the credibility of this journey was not just the endurance quality but why it had to be done. My journeys had always provided my life with some meaning, though not all its meaning.

"You think what you do has more meaning than what other people do, like the people who shuffle papers, write reports and get to where they have be on time?"

"I don't know, I never wanted to work in an office."

"Why?"

"Because I would have hated it."

"Why?"

"Ok, because it's shit when you have to be so repetitious and deal with a crap boss. I mean, there didn't seem any point in giving your life up for something that seemed not to have any meaning." I bit my lip because that was so patronising but it was too late, I'd said it.

"Let me prove to you how wrong you are, how your journey is perfectly analogous to the Myth of Sisyphus,"

"The Myth of…."

"Sisyphus… its an ancient Greek story brought up to date by the French existentialist Albert Camus. Sisyphus was a mortal who had talked Hades, the God of the Underworld, into allowing him to return temporarily to Earth but then failed to return, having felt the warmth of the sun on his body. After ignoring many warnings to come back to the Underworld he was eventually forced to return and he was given a never-ending task. His punishment was to push a

boulder *he could barely move up a hill, one slow step at a time, sweating and toiling for hours. But when he reached the top, the boulder rolled straight back down to the bottom of the hill, and he had to begin this 'journey' if you like, all over again. And so continue for all eternity."*

"I can see how hard that is and yes," I said, "I do see some comparison in the severity of his *journey* to mine, but my journey has meaning, it's not repetitious, and it doesn't bore me. In fact it fills me with satisfaction."

"Really?"

"Well, yes," although I was feeling more nervous because this thought process sounded more confident than it really was.

In the Myth of Sisyphus the massive size of the boulder merely highlights the huge effort needed to push it. Every single step is an enormous task which requires the straining of every muscle and sinew to move the boulder forward, up the hill. Yet the severity of the task merely serves to *emphasise* the tragedy. The true tragedy is the pointlessness of the journey. Anyone can attempt a meaningful task and fail to succeed. Sadness and regret may follow such failure but at least there was the chance of success. But Sisyphus's tragedy lies in the fact that the very accomplishment of his task only brings him closer to having to start all over again. So he cannot ever achieve a successful or satisfying conclusion.

"You see," said the Interviewer, *"without success of some kind you have no meaning, or rather more absurdity if this is something of which you are actually aware."*

"Count me out because, while I don't get *much* success, I do get *some*. I sometimes feel successful and that usually coincides with what others feel about my efforts, so you are wrong. But maybe I should take back what I said about filing paper; if you feel successful in whatever you do, that's justification enough." Under pressure I always reverted to supporting the underdog, because when you have been one for so long yourself, it was a natural thing to do.

"But you are wrong. Sisyphus's labour is worthless. Everything he does is without meaning, but it is worse than that."

"Why?"

Because he hates what he does. If the Gods in their divine mercy had allowed him to like what he did, whereby rolling a boulder up a hill gave him some kind of pleasure, then you would think it diminished the horror."

"That makes sense, all jobs have their issues but if you really like what you do then surely it makes more sense?" I said.

"Not at all."

The next day I took the 45 bus back into town, changed at the transit and jumped on the number 2 to Lussock Library where I could check my email on the Internet.

Jiten had sent me one detailing my financial position. It was stable. I was hanging in there. My finances were difficult, my emotional life was not easy and after being an adventurer for nearly twenty five years I sat back and wondered quite where I was up to. Apart from lots of memories, what had I achieved? I also rang London, home and New Zealand, grabbed a coffee and took the first bus that passed, jumped off at Carrs and pulled out some money at Western Union which Jiten had just transferred. I then took a bus to Don's bike shop on West Potter Street and the guys all remembered me: Don, Mike Maines, Mike number 2, Eric, everyone; it was a homecoming. For years I'd been bringing riders here on my tours, to have their bikes serviced. Mike Maines came up to me and I immediately remembered him from 2004 when I took nine riders around the world and before that, in 2002, when I brought 22 riders here doing the same thing. Mike had looked after several other Alaska expeditions plus my 31 day ride in '97 and my ride from Tierra del Fuego to here the year before that. He was Don's main mechanic and right hand man and his wife Debbie ran the spares department. Straight away he offered me a bed at his house which I gratefully accepted.

In Anchorage, Alaska
The bike arrives tomorrow (Wednesday) and Don's Motorcycle Shop is opening late to service the bike - air and oil filters, chain and sprockets and Continental Road Attack tyres. The service is scheduled for one hour with four guys working on the bike simultaneously. Then it's the crunch stage which will decide whether I get the record or not. I need to ride a minimum of 7000 miles in six days to catch up but am planning more. If I arrive in New York in 6 days' time, that leaves only 30 hours left to do to get from Madrid to Calais via Granada.

I feel strong and focused and with a revitalised bike I think I have an excellent chance to recover my title. It's been a hard journey when I have been riding - probably amongst the hardest riding I have ever done - and having to break the rhythm is also hard, but that is part of the challenge of this particular adventure.

Mike was the perfect host and was so kind. He'd lived in England when he was in the army, years ago. He really seemed to have empathised with me, partly, I think, because I brought back happy memories of his first overseas adventure as a young man.

How neatly the trappings of convention wrap themselves tightly around us, the necessary bondage of an organised society. I knew Mike would bike around the world at the drop of a hat, but, when you have no hat, no hat-stand and no where for it to fall; you begin to see the enormity of the enterprise. I had completely compromised my marriage and would have divorce papers served on me within days of getting home. A woman's heart works differently from a man's and my Anglo-Irish heart had somewhere been corrupted by the broken promise of marriage.

July 10th Anchorage, Alaska

The bike has arrived on Korean Airlines and I have the paperwork. It went via Auckland, Sydney, Seoul, China and is now, finally, in Anchorage. Customs are closed as it's a Sunday and no one is working in the warehouse but everything opens again at 08.00 Monday and it will be released during the morning. A fast service has been arranged by my mate Mike at Don's Shop. Don's a great man and his manager and main mechanic Mike has been looking after me these past days. My plan now is to ride the following itinerary of 7150 miles in less than 6 days and to arrive in New York before noon on Sunday, 17th July. The bike is already booked to fly out of the US around the 19th and I should be home by the following weekend, after finishing off the last section back to Calais, possibly via Madrid and Granada.

13th July 2005, Anchorage Alaska

I left customs at 12.30 and went straight to Don's where the service was done remarkably quickly. Tyre change, oil change, new front and rear sprockets and a new chain... all this in one hour and it solved the problem of the rumble. I left from there at 1:30 pm and then rode East to Fairbanks before turning South East towards Tok. I've just done 592 miles in 11 hours of riding, but we have to put in one hour for the service. The record clock does not stop for servicing. So I've done almost 600 miles in 12 hours. Bang on the 1200 miles-per-day schedule. It's now half past midnight and the sun has just gone down. I am now going to ride through the night to reach Dawson Creek by noon tomorrow. Dawson Creek is at the end of the Alaskan Highway. I feel really good, really focused. I realise what is really necessary and the efforts involved. This was the first half day of what is going to be 12 half days.

A few hours later...

There was lots of road construction so I couldn't manage the last 400 miles as it was late. I checked into a hotel and have started being a bit more clever in looking after myself – this is only my second hotel room on the whole trip. I'll grab four hours sleep and then be off again to catch up with my schedule. As long as I am in Salt Lake City for 09.00 Thursday I am on schedule for three 1200 mile days in a row - which means 300 miles tomorrow morning and then 1400 miles over the next 26 hours, two thirds of which is freeway with no road works. I filmed a lot today in Alaska but am not filming at all tomorrow. I'm feeling very confident. I'm on the wireless internet in my room and it's 12.30 am. I will sleep between 1am and 4am then I'll be off, when I can see what animals are out there – that's the important bit. The locals say this last part of the 'Alcan' (the Alaskan Highway) is the worst for animals and knowing when to back off is what keeps you adventuring for a long time. I'm on the verge of grabbing back 200 miles from my 1000 mile deficit. This will happen. I haven't come this far to go home empty handed.

13th July 2005

Am in Whitehorse in the Yukon - it's 12.30 pm and I've ridden 1100 miles through the night. Just had 45 minutes sleep on the side of the road and feel good for another 1200. Am 100 miles down on my best schedule but have grabbed back 200 miles off my lost time - am now only 800 miles down and am feeling stronger.

On the Alaska – Canada Highway, North America

1980 miles since yesterday, one three hour sleep and the full length of the Alaskan Highway, I found friends. Heidi and Charles who met up with me and kept me talking. They are such great mates whom I've known since my first expeditions in 1996. I usually end up on a sofa, which is better than any motel. I'm behind on my schedule so I'm going to have to ride all night to get to Salt Lake City for my tyre change; that'll teach me. It's really hard catching up stray hours at this stage in the adventure but meeting good friends, real live people who think and care about you, is the closest I get to a normal life just now, so it's important to me. But I'm late, really paranoid, got to go!

Zipped down the Alaskan Highway and through Spokane and on across the Salmon River Mountains and down to the Snake River Plain. I didn't sleep, I just rode. I didn't film and didn't look around. Sometimes there were mountains and sometimes there were trees and then desert and then Salt Lake City.

In Salt Lake City, Utah, USA

I'm at Wright's Bike Shop in Salt Lake City; great people – they are being so helpful. Tyre changed by Tim in minutes plus oil and filters. Back on the road in 40 minutes flat. Have just worked out that I have ridden a confirmed 3500 miles in 76 hours, two thirds on the Alaskan Highway and crossing the Rockies, one third on the Interstate. Tomorrow it's all Interstate, so I hope to ride 600 miles in a twelve hour period. I have actually hit the 1150 miles a day schedule; that means I have clawed back 550 miles, so now I'm only 450 miles down on the record. Have to go, more later.

It was all becoming a bit of a blur. My sleep pattern no longer existed and even though I was riding safely, I had no real idea of where I was anymore. On the outskirts of the desert area before reaching Moab I decided I'd had enough and checked into a motel. It was one of the few times I had stayed in a hotel in the middle of a ride and reminded me once again of de Maistre walking around his room, describing and memorising the furniture, their relative positions, colours and textures. In my little room the television sat against the wall and astride a small space which separated twin queen beds. The bed I'd chosen was against the wall, away from the window and slightly snugger being that few feet further from the outside world. My bed was neat while the other was strewn with the contents of my tank bag; littered with the tools and paperwork needed to continue the journey. A passport and carnet lay alongside pockets of unfolded money and gnarled bits of important paper rendered unreadable due to having had the print rubbed off by adjacent clutter. A short evening's break gave me rare time to think. As described again in 'Loneliness of the Long Distance Biker':

"Shortly after meeting Hennie in 1996 I rode the length of the Americas on a red Triumph Daytona 900cc. I started by riding from Buenos Aires to Ushuaia in Tierra del Fuego on the southernmost tip of the continent, but I fell off in snow before I even got there. I knew it was coming because the front wheel had slid three times and I'd only just managed to hold it. What on earth possessed me to think that I had the experience to ride in those conditions, on standard road tyres? Lying on the road, cushioned by the snow, looking up at the moon, in pain, I lay there blinking and sort of smiled, wondering how I was going to explain to the sponsors that it was all over before I'd even got to the start line. All I wanted was a free sports bike and it was preposterous the lengths I was prepared to go to, to get one.

I pushed on across Patagonia, and on, over the Atacama Desert under a full moon and across Peru in a surreal blaze of dawn and dusk. By the time I reached Quito I'd got Hennie out of my system. I heaved and hauled this heavy bike from corner to corner and then down the straights. I cajoled every working part to do my bidding, and mostly it did. This lump of steel and rubber and treasures of machinery helped me traverse Ecuador at night, contra los bandidos. In the rain in the Andes I slept underneath trucks by the side of the road. I was so utterly and completely disillusioned that by the time I reached the Equator, I just wanted to give up and fly home.

Deep in Colombia I was pulled off my bike by an angry mob, and that put paid to the record attempt because I missed my boat to Colon from Cartegena. It was all over. I took my foot off the gas and ambled through Panama and Nicaragua. I skirted El Salvador. I wanted so much to go into the cowboy country and play Russian roulette with my life, but by some fluke of sensible judgment I played safe and instead took back-roads and stream-beds across Guatemala and Honduras. I raced across the full length of Mexico to San Antonio. I slept under a table while my bike was being serviced and set off again to ride through the night. I rode and I rode because I didn't know what else to do. I had a mission and I needed some girl's handkerchief attached to my lance. I was quite simply some fucking manic Don Quixote figure going quietly mad all by myself. I was talking to myself in my helmet for weeks at a time so it was no wonder I was getting good at dealing with loneliness and the absurd. In the end I rode from Tierra del Fuego to Alaska in 30 days but I had failed miserably to beat the 19 day car record. As a record attempt it was a disaster and I told no one about it, but, as a training run, it had been a success. I was, after all, still alive and even though my ankle was still a bit stiff, my bike riding had improved a lot.

★ ★ ★ ★ ★

I'd had just five hours of much needed sleep since Anchorage. I didn't know it then, but other than a few brief 10 minute power naps, I would not sleep again until Toronto. By now I was truly appreciating what I needed to do to regain those lost thousand miles. The thousand miles that India had cost me. The same figure that haunted my every move ever since the project was conceived years ago. This journey was above all an attempt to beat the 2002 motorcycle record that had been so tightly scheduled that to crack it I was going to need everything I could muster, in energy, riding ability, organisation and sheer pig-headed will power. Now, every single hour counted. There was no room for error or movement away from this schedule and to ride any more than 1150 miles a day would mean riding without sleep for days at a time. It is still a shock to me that I was able to ride this whole North American section with only seven hours' sleep. This did not seem possible at the time, yet it happened. It was never part of my plan. It would have seemed absurd before the start yet here I was, at the end of a near 7000 mile journey ridden in 146 and a half hours. And whatever weather and terrain appeared just had to be ridden through – there was no slowing down in the gravel on the Alcan; no roadworks were allowed to impede the schedule; nor did the rain that fell so heavily. There was such a solid curtain of water that I wanted to reach out and part it with my hand.

I was also tiring. It had rained heavily for a thousand miles and while it wasn't cold, it added resistance against my progress through the air that my weakening body had to overcome. In the traffic during the day, plumes of spray obscured everything beyond a twenty metre radius around me and ironically, the busier the route, the less traffic I could actually see. If there was a pile up ahead I would not know until it was too late. If I went down I would certainly be driven over by following traffic. From what I'd seen of North American car drivers, very few would have the ability to take avoiding action. The size of the roads and lumbering nature of most of the vehicles did not provide people with the need for, or any practice of, thinking and reacting quickly. There are stories of motorcycle victims surviving a fall on the interstate only to be run over and killed by ten vehicles that failed to brake. Slow reaction time makes for murderous roads.

Indian drivers wave wildly and want to chat as you pass whereas Americans stare straight ahead with a look that suggests they'd prefer it if you weren't there. With their rebellious clothing adorned with patches and their *de rigueur* bandanas, motorcyclists here present a more intimidating presence than their European counterparts. On bikes the size of small cars, the greasy biker brigade have long since been replaced by middle aged people trying to recreate a time in their life when the surfer / biker look represented freedom. I spoke to very few, but they were there, hundreds of them, in their little gangs.

The rain continued to fall and I had to work hard not to slow down or stop and shelter. In the short term, the easiest thing to do would be to stop and take the slower, safer course home. The long term implications of my not getting this record were more personally damaging and it had crossed my mind that should I fail, I would think about retiring completely and accept that I had done enough. The rain was eroding any time I had made up the previous night and after such a huge effort that spanned this massive continent, it was not acceptable to watch my lead slip away, so I just rode and fuelled and rode. I had stopped filming because the very observation of this journey had begun to affect the outcome. By spending so much time recording the event, I'd forced myself into having to ride harder. Too much observation meant a faster riding pattern to compensate for a failing schedule. Too little observation kept the project invisible and diminished the evidence available to verify the record. The tactics required to record this moment of micro history without affecting the result were finely balanced. All day it rained. Countless corporate branded eateries gave me no clue to where I was. Interstate America is the same in Sacramento as in Santa Fe. The rain seemed endless and I began to wonder if it would ever stop and if I would have to suffer it all the way to Toronto.

Thoughts in a helmet can revolve around a single idea for hours. Ideas that have no escape can sometimes go rotten. Locked as they are in head protection, they start off as fresh as any new thought, but ricocheting off solid surfaces become brittle and, like bad breath and poor humour, can become stale. It was like that the first time, except somehow then, there were more moments than I have now to examine why I do what I do.

Fastest Man Extract (Alaska 1997)

The easy way would have been to describe this journey as one of physical troughs and bumps - you know, where I ate, where I tinkered with the engine, reciting adventures from some 'Boy's Own' story. How I escaped with a bullet lodged in my head. But I'm through with that. I've come out the other side." I was trying too hard to explain myself. My head was hurting with these inane conversations. Outside, the wind whipped up and the cherry blossom rained down in clusters. In my dream I was knee-deep in blossom and knew that if I stayed there long enough, I would be buried in it and would suffocate. This journey was all about time. Time to ride and time to rest. A time to fart, a time to bleat. Every minute of my reality prescribed in linear form.

For twelve hours the rain fell without a break. Big cities came and went; Gallup, Albuquerque, San Antonio and a near straight line from Houston to Toronto. The rain and the trashy outskirts of most North American cities made me think of Roy's dying soliloquy in the film *Bladerunner;* I think it's one of the most moving in cinematic history. Against all the odds, in a really rank place, an emotionally receptive android is literally hanging on to life by his finger tips: *'I've seen things you people wouldn't believe. I've watched attack ships on fire off the shoulder of Orion. I've watched sea-beams dance by the Tannhäuser gate. Now all these moments will be lost in time, like tears in rain. Time to die.'*

Likewise, I've seen the vertical walls of ice fields retreating under a midnight sun and listened in a desert so silent I could hear the blood rushing through my veins and the clip of pocket valves flip back into place. The great places where sea-beams dance and senses are made with colour were beyond my navigation that night as I held my own against a forest of brake-lights that came into view all around me, piercing the dense spray like glow crimson glow-worms. At last, I made it to Toronto and went straight to the freighters.

Toronto, Canada.

I have never felt so pleased with my biking performance as I do now. In just over six days I have ridden from Anchorage, down the full length of the Alaskan Highway and then descended across the USA to the Mexican border. Then from El Paso to San Antonio I headed in a straight line to Toronto - 6800 miles. Due to the terrorist bombings in London, New York customs had advised me that my bike might be held for up to two weeks before it would be allowed it to fly and suggested it might be quicker from Canada. Fortunately they were right and the bike flew to Lisbon the very next day. The ride really hadn't been easy. From Monday 12.30 till now, (sometime Sunday Central Time), I have had seven hours of proper sleep. The rest has been cat naps – as soon as my head hits my tank bag I am sleep astride my bike in seconds; that is how tired I have become. More than this, today I started falling asleep while I was actually riding. Every few minutes I would fade out and for a brief few seconds I would be riding the bike asleep on the highway. I have a strange awareness it's happening, but not initially. For the first two or three seconds I am out for the count – just sitting, balancing , holding the accelerator grip firmly but well asleep. And then I wake up, catch the bike just before it starts to veer off somewhere and carry on. It's a type of madness that a lot of motorcyclists will understand; I don't know if anyone else does. This has been amongst my hardest ever riding. I will get this record by a few hundred miles and a few hours, but right now it is head to head almost to the hour. I'm too tired to write any more.

Toronto

After leaving the bike with Hassain at the freighters I took the bus to Terminal 3 nearby. Money was tight and I was tired so I found out which part of the airport would be a quiet place to hang out for the night and duly sourced a cheap one way ticket to New York. Andrew was the driver operating the inter-terminal shuttle and he drove me to a corner of the airport where West Jet were relocating so no one went there just now, apart from the floor cleaners. Unfortunately, tonight was floor cleaning night.

Diary Toronto Airport Tuesday 19th July

About to check in with Canjet, Canada's budget airline. Feeling a rare mixture of fear and elation. The Chairman of Mobil said to me when I finished my 31 day journey in 1997 that you have to enjoy what small successes you have because they happen very rarely, and he was so right. It has been a long time since I felt professionally contented with something that I have done. Yet, already I have built up in my mind that nothing is going to happen when I get back and as soon as I return it'll be straight down to work in the office, pick up the kids from their mum in Spain, look after them myself for August and write a book, make a film then finish off preparations to take 12 riders on the first stage of their round the world tour to the Iranian border. There is very little time to reflect on the journey. The end is rushing into view. What was an all-consuming journey, which has held my focus in a stranglehold, is soon going to release me from its grip. Never before have I experienced such a powerful force from a journey. I never thought that would ever happen to me again as strongly as this, but it did.

I flew into La Guardia and went straight to the Virgin Atlantic check-in desk and asked if I could hang about the clubhouse and drink lots of Margaritas. They said yes, so I did. Then I was on the plane, squished between everyone as we shuffled down the aisle, until I noticed I had the only free four-seat row to myself. Hmmm the party continues. I had to pinch myself because nothing was in the bag. In my hazy margarita-fuelled head I reckoned I was about even on miles and time, maybe advantage to me. I wasn't sure and had stopped being concerned about it. I had begun to recognise what the journey was in isolation. I knew I was ahead. The overtake had been swift indeed. Once I was surer of my ground, I would do exactly what was needed but nothing more. I wanted to cruise to a safe margin rather than risk everything by doing something silly.

THE LAST LEG

I flew into Lisbon before the weekend about the same time as the bike. The original plan was to fly the bike from New York but instead we had to divert to Toronto because of the bomb blasts in London and the subsequent tightening of security in the US. Sometimes, last minute decisions, effectively carried out, can turn out well. There was no way I could know how long I'd be on the road so an exit date from North America couldn't be planned in advance. After dropping off the bike one last time with the freighters, I flew immediately to Lisbon where I was met by some new friends who had read about me on my website. Augusto took me out for dinner and introduced me to bikers who were keen to meet me. It was a charming gesture and much appreciated because at this point I was feeling really alone.

The bike arrived the next day and Augusto and Paolo helped me to get the bike out of customs for the final time. Paolo and his friend decided to accompany me and we rode fast to the border with Spain. As is the wont of bikers, we promised to be friends for ever. Once in Spain I discovered that my Visa card had finally packed up and that I had less than £80 to get me back to England. Fortunately, thanks to the generosity of Dave 'Z Power' Marsden, a ferry ticket was waiting for me in Dunkirk, but that was over 1500 miles away. As things stood, I was about to lose the record due to simply running out of money. Being a Saturday it was impossible to have cash easily transferred – it seemed as if the god of pound notes and other common currencies was beginning to conspire against me. I had a disastrous inability to hold on to money I'd earned over the years and yet, like many catastrophes and disasters, most of my financial crises could have been avoided with just a little forward planning,

In a brief 'phone conversation with my soon-to-be ex-wife, she said she'd ask her mum (who lives in Spain) if I could borrow my petrol money from her but insisted that I apologise for writing about her in the way I had in my last book. I refused and said I'd rather chew off my tongue than compromise my artistic integrity by censoring something that I didn't even think was offensive. She said she'd ask anyway. Beatrice was the only person who could help me. She lived near Valencia on the east coast of Spain, which wasn't exactly on the way from Madrid to Paris, but fortunately it wasn't too much of a detour either. By the strangest twist of fate, my soon-to-be ex-mother in law was going to rescue my record attempt.

So I rode hard across the brown landscape of Spain to Madrid. The weather was dry and bright but the traffic from the Spanish capital was thick and slow due to large numbers of people escaping to the coast for the weekend. I rode for hour after hour and arrived at Beatrice's cottage at eleven o'clock in the evening. She was there with her husband Richard and made me a cup of tea. Dear woman handed over the money, 200 euros, which was enough to get me home. That meant I could still get the record; that, after so many days and months of feverish preparation and riding, years of thinking about it, precious plans forming in my head, my own hopes and those of my sponsors, my friends and my family, would not be dashed.

I thanked Beatrice for the cash and the tea and scarpered. I rode right through the night, across the border and on up the length of France, stopping only for fuel. After recalculating my start and finish from Paris I had ridden 19 650 miles around the world in 463 hours and 15 minutes, 45 minutes ahead of the 19 day 8 hour record held by the rider and his pillion and 13 days faster than the solo record I set in 1997. Had I continued to Calais I would have accumulated too many miles and lost too much time and the record would have been put in jeopardy. By moving the start and finish of the record to Paris I had snatched back the title of 'fastest man around the world'. Did it matter? Yes and no. No, because like all such expeditions it was deeply foolish to have put my life at risk for something so naively egotistical. Yes, because as a small example of how the human spirit can make itself heard above the din of mediocrity, it had struck a chord. Everyone likes to be heard but some of us need a different platform on which to stand. Then, when everyone has gone away and it's all been filed away and forgotten, I can sit in a warm glow of satisfaction and happiness, at least for a while.

If you would like to ride with Nick on one of his tours
please check out his website:

www.motochallenge.com

Nick Sanders' Motorcycle Diaries
vol 2

DVDs FROM NICK SANDERS FILMS

Length: 1hr
Price: £10

Length: 90mins
Price: £10

BOOKS FROM
ON THE ROAD
PUBLISHING

Price: £7.95

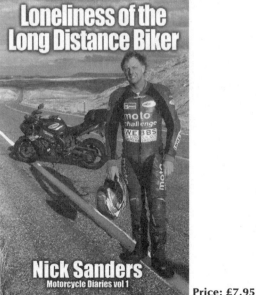

Price: £7.95